D.T. Lahey

D.T. Lahey is a retired Ontario teacher and department head of English. Lahey's interest in genealogy led to research of Sir George Simpson's origins, his wives, and his children. He has published articles breaking new ground in Simpson research in *Families: The Journal of the Ontario Genealogical Society*, and lives in Guelph, Ontario.

In the same collection

Ven Begamudré, *Isaac Brock: Larger Than Life*
Lynne Bowen, *Robert Dunsmuir: Laird of the Mines*
Kate Braid, *Emily Carr: Rebel Artist*
Kathryn Bridge, *Phyllis Munday: Mountaineer*
Edward Butts, *Henry Hudson: New World Voyager*
William Chalmers, *George Mercer Dawson: Geologist, Scientist, Explorer*
Anne Cimon, *Susanna Moodie: Pioneer Author*
Deborah Cowley, *Lucille Teasdale: Doctor of Courage*
Gary Evans, *John Grierson: Trailblazer of Documentary Film*
Julie H. Ferguson, *James Douglas: Father of British Columbia*
Judith Fitzgerald, *Marshall McLuhan: Wise Guy*
lian goodall, *William Lyon Mackenzie King: Dreams and Shadows*
Tom Henighan, *Vilhjalmur Stefansson: Arctic Adventurer*
Stephen Eaton Hume, *Frederick Banting: Hero, Healer, Artist*
Naïm Kattan, *A.M. Klein: Poet and Prophet*
Betty Keller, *Pauline Johnson: First Aboriginal Voice of Canada*
Heather Kirk, *Mazo de la Roche: Rich and Famous Writer*
Valerie Knowles *William C. Van Horne: RailwayTitan*
Vladimir Konieczny, *Glenn Gould: A Musical Force*
Michelle Labrèche-Larouche, *Emma Albani: International Star*
Wayne Larsen, *A.Y. Jackson: A Love for the Land*
Wayne Larsen, *James Wilson Morrice: Painter of Light and Shadow*
Wayne Larsen, *Tom Thomson: Artist of the North*
Francine Legaré, *Samuel de Champlain: Father of New France*
Margaret Macpherson, *Nellie McClung: Voice for the Voiceless*
Nicholas Maes, *Robertson Davies: Magician of Words*
Dave Margoshes, *Tommy Douglas: Building the New Society*
Marguerite Paulin, *René Lévesque: Charismatic Leader*
Raymond Plante, *Jacques Plante: Behind the Mask*
Jim Poling Sr., *Tecumseh: Shooting Star, Crouching Panther*
T.F. Rigelhof, *George Grant: Redefining Canada*
Tom Shardlow, *David Thompson: A Trail by Stars*
Arthur Slade, *John Diefenbaker: An Appointment with Destiny*
Roderick Stewart, *Wilfrid Laurier: A Pledge for Canada*
Sharon Stewart, *Louis Riel: Firebrand*
André Vanasse, *Gabrielle Roy: A Passion for Writing*
John Wilson, *John Franklin: Traveller on Undiscovered Seas*
John Wilson, *Norman Bethune: A Life of Passionate Conviction*
Rachel Wyatt, *Agnes Macphail: Champion of the Underdog*

A QUEST BIOGRAPHY

GEORGE SIMPSON

BLAZE OF GLORY

D.T. LAHEY

DUNDURN PRESS
TORONTO

Editor: Allison Hirst
Design: Jesse Hooper
Printer: Marquis

Library and Archives Canada Cataloguing in Publication

Lahey, Dale, 1933-
    George Simpson : blaze of glory / by D.T. Lahey.

(A Quest biography)
Includes bibliographical references and index.
Issued also in an electronic format.
ISBN 978-1-55488-773-6

    1. Simpson, George, Sir, 1792?-1860. 2. Hudson's Bay Company--Biography.
3. Northwest, Canadian--Biography. 4. Hudson's Bay Company--History--19th
century. 5. Northwest, Canadian--History--To 1870. 6. Northwest,
Canadian--Discovery and exploration. 7. Fur trade--Canada--History--19th
century. I. Title. II. Series: Quest biography

FC3213.1.S5L34 2010   971.2'01092   C2010-902698-5

1   2   3   4   5   15   14   13   12   11

Conseil des Arts du Canada   Canada Council for the Arts   Canada   ONTARIO ARTS COUNCIL CONSEIL DES ARTS DE L'ONTARIO

We acknowledge the support of the **Canada Council for the Arts** and the **Ontario Arts Council** for our publishing program. We also acknowledge the financial support of the **Government of Canada** through the **Canada Book Fund** and **Livres Canada Books,** and the **Government of Ontario** through the **Ontario Book Publishers Tax Credit** program, and the **Ontario Media Development Corporation.**

www.dundurn.com

Dundurn Press
3 Church Street, Suite 500
Toronto, Ontario, Canada
M5E 1M2

Gazelle Book Services Limited
White Cross Mills
High Town, Lancaster, England
LA1 4XS

Dundurn Press
2250 Military Road
Tonawanda, NY
U.S.A. 14150

To my son
Neil Stewart Lahey
for everything

Contents

Author's Note

The Dundurn Quest Library series presents short, readable biographies of Canadian historical personages, for young or new readers. The intent is to provide fresh estimates of a historical person's life and achievement. A new look at George Simpson is timely. Recent writers seem more concerned with presenting sensational, semi-fictional accounts of the man's life based more on fancy than fact. To avoid this, I have returned to the beginning, letting Simpson tell his own story in his own words as much as possible. Simpson was a powerful, exhilarating writer, so this approach should let the reader see him as he was, not as he has been previously represented.

In a short biography of this sort, it is not possible to touch on everything that Simpson accomplished in his forty-year tenure of power. Enough should be offered, however, that the reader will be encouraged to go to the further reading section at the end of this volume.

If the reader finds that George Simpson seems to have been always on the move, that is exactly true. He governed by travelling, and if we are to be true to his life, we must dutifully follow him on those travels.

This biography will introduce the reader to Simpson's round-the-world journey of 1841/42 — a neglected source. It presents some of Simpson's best insights into his own governance, yet still offers much "perilous adventure" to whet the reader's interest after more than 160 years.

The quoted material in this book has been transcribed without editing for spelling and capitalization. Some punctuation was added, however, to improve the clarity of the text. I have chosen to use Imperial measure instead of metric throughout as this was the system in place in Simpson's time.

Special vocabulary and abbreviations

Committee The Governor and Committee in London, the final authority

Company The Hudson's Bay Company

Council The Council of the Northern Department, Simpson's governing body in Rupert's Land. Simpson was accountable to it, and the Council was accountable to the Committee.

HBC Hudson's Bay Company

NWC North West Company

Union The amalgamation of the HBC and the NWC in 1821

Prologue: A Gentleman in Waiting

London, 23d. Feby 1820
To: Mr. and Mrs. Pooler, My old Friend Dick,
Miss Helen,*
Reigate, Surrey, England

Since I last had the pleasure of seeing You, an unexpected circumstance has occurred which renders it necessary for me to leave Old England for a time, and at the short notice of 5 days.

On Sunday afternoon I leave Town for Liverpool, embark in the packet for New York on Tuesday, from thence proceed direct for Montreal and afterward take an inland Rout

---

* The Pooler family had lived In London and had recently moved to Reigate, south of the City. Dick was their young son, and his head was full of adventure stories. The other children were Miss Helen and twins who were aged about six in 1820.

by the St. Lawrence, Lakes Ontario, Huron, Superior, and Winnipeg to Hudson Bay and afterward to Athapascow to Slave Lake and Copper Mine River. The Journey is rather a serious undertaking and the mission is important connected with the affairs of Lord Selkirk, the Hudson's Bay and North West Compys. Travellers you know meet with some extraordinary adventures I shall therefore have some wonderful Tales to relate when I again have the pleasure of visiting You.

Pray offer my affectionate regard to Mrs. and Miss Pooler Dick and the Children as also to Mrs. Palmer and with unfeigned esteem believe me always to be

My Dear Sir
Yours Most Truly
Geo. Simpson

* * *

Montreal 28th Apl. 1820
To: Same

I am sure it will not be uninteresting to learn that I have got this length in perfect safety and in the enjoyment of good Health and spirits.

My adventures hitherto possess little interest, yet I shall give you a summary account of my

proceeding since my departure from London,
and by the time I shall next have the pleasure
of seeing you my Journal will be furnished
with abundant store for a long evengs chat. On
the 27 Feby I left Town for Liverpool where
I was detained a few Days by contrary winds,
and on the 4th ultimo embarked on board the
James Monroe for New York: my Fellow passengers consisted of 13 gentlemen & 2 Ladies;
the Spanish Ambassador Genl. Vevas and suite
were of the party, the other Gentlemen were
commercial Men, but amongst them were two
Vile Radicals who would have kept us in con-
tinual discord during the Voyage had we not
sent them to Coventry which was affected not
only by threats but by actual hard thumps. Of
the ladies ... they were of the same cast going
to join their husbands who by their treason-
able proceedings had found it necessary to take
refuge in the states, an asylum for the outcasts
and malcontents of all Nations.... On the whole
we had a very agreeable party but the passage
throughout was one continued storm; on the
banks of Newfoundland we encountered very
severe Weather and [were] much annoyed with
Ice; the wind was so intense that wherever the
spray reached, it immediately congealed, the
Deck covered with Ice a foot thick and our sails
as thick as a 3 Inch plank; with some difficulty
however we got out of this Frozen Latitude and
on the 4th instant landed at New York after a

quick but tempestuous voyage of 31 Days. The
harbour of New York is perhaps the finest in
the World, protected by strong batteries so as to
render it impregnable from the sea. The Town
is well laid out, some handsome streets and a
few elegant publick buildings; it is situated on
an island formed by the harbour the North and
East Rivers and is altogether a gay, bustling city
with a population of about 130,000 Souls.

At New York I remained but a few days
and received much attention & hospitality
from some friends to whom I had Letters of
Introduction. From thence I took my departure
inland by Steamer to Albany about 170 Miles
up the North River which is a noble stream navigable by Ships of any burthen and an average
of from 1/2 to 3/4ths of a mile broad on which
there is much Traffick & abounding with fish....

Albany is a neat pretty town where I merely
remained an hour to get horses and proceeded
direct for this place, thro' boundless Forests,
extensive plains and over some stupendous
Mountains; an interesting country at any other
Season of the Year but covered with snow the
roads one continued morass so that it was
necessary to keep my eye fixed on them to
avoid getting drowned in the Sea of Mud and
the weather so bad that I had no opportunity
of devoting much of my attention to the sur-
rounding Scenery; my vehicle was nothing
more than an open cart drawn by 4 animalcule

unworthy the Name of Horses and after about 50 Spills in which I had numerous bruises & contusions was compelled to have recourse to the Marrowbone stage the greater part of the Journey; my time being limited I found it necessary to Travel by forced marches 19 hours out of the 24 and got here the seventh Day nearly worn out with Fatigue; had the credit of opening the St. Lawrence being the first boat that crossed this Season, the floating Ice made it a source of some danger but the Soaking I had will teach me to be more cautious in future. Here I am in excellent quarters and quite at Home with many of the first Families in Town; my time pleasantly divided between business and amusement; Dinner parties, Tea Squalls, Cards, Balls, Theatres & Masquerades occupy my evengs, and I assure you the representative of the Hudsons Bay Coy & Lord Selkirk is looked upon as no inconsiderate personage in this part of the World.

I am busily preparing for my Journey into the interior, a serious undertaking, my conveyance is a canoe pulled by 10 stout Fellows which they carry over the portages; my Cloak will answer all the purposes of a bed and the canoe turned bottom upwards my chamber so that there is no danger of my getting enervated by ease & luxury. The first part of my Journey I expect to accomplish in 40 Days and my future proceedings will be regulated by the

state of things in the interior. The serious dif-
ferences between the Hudsons Bay & North
West Compys are the causes of my mission and
from the preparation being made by both parties I suspect we shall have some hard Blows; I
am not however paid for fighting will therefore
keep my bones whole if possible yet show my
Governors that I am not wanting for Courage if
necessity puts it to the test. There is a possibility that I may be obstructed in my Rout as the
N.W. Coy, a band of unprincipled and Lawless
Marauders, stick at nothing however desperate
to gain their ends; I am, however, armed to the
Teeth, will sell my Life if in danger as dear as
possible and never allow a north Wester [to]
come within reach of my Riffle if Flint Steel and
bullet can keep him off.

My best regards and with unfeigned esteem
believe me to be

My dear Sir
Yours most truly and Sincerely
Geo. Simpson

These letters reveal the quintessential George Simpson. He has just
been promoted on short notice to the position of governor *locum
tenens* of the Hudson's Bay Company (HBC); that is, to take charge
of the Company's interests in North America if the appointed governor is arrested. This Simpson is young, good-natured, almost
boyish. He is brash, bright, quick to adverse judgments of whole

groups (Americans, Northwesters — judgments he is just as quick to reverse), quick to put his fists to work, and a lucid writer and describer. He revels in the toils of travel, storms at sea, oceans of mud, and the danger of crossing a river in ice flood. He loves good company, banquets and balls, good food, dancing, and cards. He is an affable, social man. Awed by his sudden rise of fortune, but enjoying the attention, he is still a little uncertain about his ability to carry out his new duties or to show the courage necessary to meet a fearless enemy.

In just over a year he will govern a quarter of the North American continent.

1

Dingwall:
Search for Scottish Origins

*Communicate with me in one of the
unknown tongues.*
— George Simpson

The town of Dingwall, in northern Scotland, lies enclosed on the north and south by two high hills, but on the east the vista opens onto the Cromarty Firth (inlet), and to the west the road leads into the western Highlands. In the 1790s, as well as now, the *Statistical Account of Scotland* tells us: "Every traveller is struck by the natural beauty of the country."

The sea cuts deeply into the landscape in several long firths — Dornoch, Cromarty, Moray, Beauly — opening glistening vistas of water to complement the rolling headlands. To the north, Ben Wyvis, one of Scotland's highest peaks, is always covered in snow, even in the hottest days of summer. From Fodderty in Strathpeffer, looking eastward, "the valley has a commanding view of the town and parish of Dingwall," which "forms a beautiful interchange of hill and valley, wood and water, corn fields and meadows." And beyond, the glistening firth wends its way to the North Sea, conjuring visions of far-off places at the ends of the world.

To find a place as far north in Canada we must think of Churchill, Manitoba. But the air at Dingwall is warmed by the gulf current, making the land warm and arable, the landscape shaped by centuries of agriculture.

Here in this lush beautiful landscape, George Simpson was born, probably in the early spring of 1792. But where exactly he was born — in the town or in the nearby countryside — remains uncertain.

His father was George Simpson senior, born in 1759 in the fishing village of Avoch (pronounced *ach* to rhyme with *loch*) about nine miles east of Dingwall. George Sr.'s father was the Church of Scotland minister, the Reverend Thomas Simpson. His mother was Isobel Mackenzie of the powerful clan of the Mackenzies of Kintail.

About 1775, George Sr. finished his schooling and a position was found for him in Dingwall as a writer's apprentice. He became a lawyer in the Sheriff Courts in the town and a factor for lairds in the nearby countryside.

In 1805 he was recommended by several local landowners to the position of agent for the British Fisheries Society at Ullapool, north of Dingwall. The governor of the company supported him through to his retirement. The secretary of the society, however, thought he spent too much of his time communicating with the settlers. He was a deeply religious man, sprinkling his letters with religious sentiments: "I am able to thank my God for all His Mercies.... It is with a grateful heart I acknowledge the Goodness of the Lord.... [May] the all-powerful Protector ... guard & watch over you."

Certainly he adored his son, referring to him as "My dearest beloved George." The picture that emerges from these brief glimpses is that of a rather decent man, pleasant, friendly, and warm-hearted, a devout Christian and adoring father. If he had a fault, perhaps it was that his professional responsibility was compromised by his compassion for the poor. The question we have to ask is how such a man might have responded to the unexpected arrival of a son.

In October 1789 George Sr. would have celebrated his thirtieth birthday. By then, it would seem, he was settled into a quiet bachelorhood. However, in the next year and a half his life was turned topsy-turvy, and by the spring of 1791 he had fallen for the charms of a young woman, and had fathered a child — a love child, legend has it, born with great intellect and wit.

It is said that nothing is known of George's mother. But that is not quite true. Some evidence leads to reasonable assumptions. For instance, George's cousins, Thomas and Alexander Simpson, who later grew up in Dingwall, both sneered at George's lowly birth. The father was not of lowly birth, so the cousins must have been talking about the mother. It's entirely possible that she was from what was then called the "lower classes," which included farmers, crofters, mechanics, and servants, most of whom lived in the country. Those of the so-called "upper classes" — lawyers, ministers, merchants, and gentry — lived, for the most part, in the towns.

A relationship crossing class lines shouldn't surprise us. Gentlemen were having children by country women at such a steady rate that ministers of the Scottish church spent much of their time tracking them down to make them pay for the welfare of the mother and child. There is no record, however, of George Sr.'s appearance before a kirk session or presbytery, where matters of illegitimacy were dealt with.

Lower class, of course, is a label given to working people by those considering themselves upper class. Genetically it is by no means an inferior status. This was certainly true of the mother, who left her genetic imprint on her child for all to see. George grew into a man at least two inches, perhaps as much as four inches, taller than the average men of his generation. He had blue eyes and red hair — unmistakable Celtic characteristics. As an adult he had a barrel chest, legendary stamina, and a stability of character that did not come from his father, whose family is described as delicate of frame and health. But no one ever accused George of being delicate. Certainly George's mother was, judging from George himself, someone in considerable physical contrast to the delicate Simpson family, into which, in this case, one must argue that the infusion of new blood was a good thing. We might expect, then, that Simpson's mother was a strong, healthy, intelligent woman who shared with her son that red hair and eye brightly blue, a woman whose natural affection could only be heightened by a child bearing so many of her Celtic characteristics.

Another distinction separated the classes in those days: English was rapidly replacing Gaelic as the preferred language spoken by the upper classes. The Simpson family from which George Sr. came, spoke English. The lower classes still spoke Gaelic. So if George's mother was from the lower classes, the odds are that she spoke Gaelic, could not read or write, and knew little, if any, English.

As it happens, George could speak Gaelic as if it was his first language, and it may well have been. We know that because he later tells us so. This was no smattering of the language picked up in the schoolyard. He spoke it well enough to converse in it for months at a time, and to translate from it when necessary. All this suggests that young George spent his early years in the country. He would have learned his Gaelic at his mother's knee, playing with the country boys, and listening to the Gaelic-speaking adults around him.

Far from being neglected in such an environment, young George would have been favourably privileged. He was, after all, the factor's son, the son of that warm-hearted, friendly, gregarious, compassionate, and religious man, who also had blood links to the Mackenzies of Kintail. In such circumstances, he and his son would have been accorded all the deference to which their positions entitled them — George Sr. as factor and George Jr. as factor's son.

On whatever estate he spent his childhood, he would have lived in the factor's house. Young George may have played with the country boys, but he stood on a higher social plane. His life would have been lived not only in the simplicity of a country setting, but in the knowledge that he was the factor's son and a Mackenzie scion. This special standing in his world later translated into that easy command he displayed in Rupert's Land.

Somehow, in his young mind, he would have picked up a good understanding of the common people among whom he lived. The writers of *The Statistical Account* all agree that the country people were, on the whole, a sober and decent people, whose peccadilloes, when they occurred, were noted in an apologetic, even forgiving way:

> The people in general are sober and quiet,
> but when an opportunity occurs, such as at a

wedding, or even a funeral, it cannot be denied that some of them occasionally exceed the bounds of perfect moderation.... They cannot be entirely acquitted of poaching in game or salmon; nor is the country entirely free from the degrading and demoralizing practice of smuggling whisky.

Later, in Rupert's Land, George would find a people not much different from these country folk, and provide them with a way of life that included a great deal of freedom.

George Sr. must have been nonplussed when he discovered he had fathered a child. Gentlemen often took such children into their protection and provided them with a good education, while a suitable husband was found for the woman in her own class. But marriage between a gentleman and a country woman rarely occurred. However, in this case, George senior defied the rule — he married the mother.

Marriage, of course, exists in many forms. Sometimes it is sanctioned by a church, sometimes by a civil authority. Sometimes it is an exchange of vows between the partners before witnesses. Sometimes it is by cohabitation and repute — that is, if the parties are *seen* to be living together as man and wife, then they *are* man and wife. In Scotland, if a child is conceived out of wedlock, and later the man and woman marry, the child is legitimate.

Alexander Simpson claimed that George was an illegitimate child, and this has been believed and repeated by many people. But Alexander is giving us hearsay evidence, not eyewitness evidence. In any case, his testimony is wrong, because we have an eyewitness that claims otherwise. In 1851, a man named Hugh Munro wrote to Sir George:

> Death has made sad havoc amongst my friends and relations since I had the pleasure of address- ing you last.... I really feel as if I were left alone, different days, to when I passed a fortnight with your respected father and mother in Dingwall.

Taken at face value, Munro is giving us clear evidence that George Sr. and the mother were married by cohabitation and repute. And there is good reason to believe that the marriage may have been contracted in a church: it is difficult to imagine that George Simpson, a devoutly Christian man, would have left his son unbaptized — or, for that matter, with the stigma of ille- gitimacy hanging over him. If George had turned for help within the church, he could look no further than to his half-brother William, missionary minister to the Strathconon, just two miles south of Dingwall. William could have performed the marriage ceremony for his brother, but his registers have not survived. We can't be sure what happened then, but marriage by cohabitation and repute seems likely. Marriage with church sacraments also remains a distinct possibility.

What became of the mother, we don't know. George Sr. retired from the British Fisheries Society in 1829 and moved to the village of Redcastle, where he lived out his days. In 1841 he speaks of his blindness and other ailments that kept him bedridden. He appears in the Scotland 1841 census, his age rounded to eighty. A few months later George Sr. would have celebrated his eighty-second birthday. No burial record exists to confirm his date of death.

Courtesy of the author.

Rivulet Cottage, Redcastle by Beauly, Scotland, the last home of George Simpson Sr.

* * *

At some point, perhaps at about the age of six (1798), young George moved to Dingwall. We know that George Sr. was in Dingwall in 1805. We know that George Jr. attended school in Dingwall. And we know that Mrs. Simpson was in Dingwall, because Munro saw her there. In the early 1800s, in all likelihood, George would have lived in Dingwall with his mother and father.

In 1791 the town of Dingwall held only 745 souls, but the sparse population belied its importance to the North Country. Of the three boroughs in Ross-shire, "Dingwall is accordingly by much the most flourishing." Six lawyers made the Dingwall

Sheriff Court the busiest in the county. Seven merchants, sixty mechanics, and twenty apprentices gave the impression of great industry for a town consisting principally of one long street.

For young George Dingwall it would have presented quite a different life from that in the quiet countryside. The language of the streets, the homes, the school, and the kirk was English. So George had to master the language — one so very different from the one he had been speaking that he never quite lost his Gaelic speech patterns.

The school held between sixty and eighty students — the children of local mechanics, farmers, and townspeople. The playground would have provided Simpson with a broad cross-section of social classes to associate with. Their names can be learned from the parish records of baptism — surnames such as Baine, Fraser, MacKay, McDonald, McLeod, Munro, Stewart, and Tomlie. All would have been known to George, some would have been his friends; some swam with him, some trekked the hills with him. But only Aemilius Simpson, the son

The village of Avoch. The spire of the church where Sir George Simpson's grandfather was the minister can be seen on the hill in the distance.

of schoolmaster Alexander Simpson, is mentioned by George by name — the only reference that definitely places George in Dingwall.

In town, young George would have come under the influence of his grandmother, Isobel Mackenzie, the widow of the Reverend Thomas Simpson. She lived in Dingwall from 1787 until her death in 1821, aged ninety. She was there from the time of George Simpson's birth until the time he left for Rupert's Land.

She was a vigorous woman in her sixties and seventies when young George lived there, and she was no ordinary minister's wife. At her death she was described as

> uniformly conscientious in the discharge of all of her social and relative duties; at the same time a peculiar suavity of manners and prepossessing address, secured her the love and esteem of all who knew her. She was a sincere and devout Christian, humble, modest, and unassuming. The influence of religion on her mind was discernible, from the sweetness of her temper, and the benevolence of her heart. To her own family she was endeared by the most affectionate ties; she was beloved in life.

From the description, Isobel was a formidable woman who could only have had a profound influence on her grandson. George was the first grandchild to come into her life. He would have filled a special place in her sense of generations. She held the family lore and would have related it to young George. So he likely spent his Dingwall days imbued with a sense of Mackenzie power and authority distilled through his grandmother. There was a long line of greatness in her descent, and she probably let people know it.

The ancient schoolhouse that George Simpson attended still stands in Dingwall, on the High Street. The schoolmaster in George's time was Alexander Simpson, no relation, except that he courted George's Aunt Mary from 1793 to 1807, when they finally married. During the courtship, Alexander must often have been in Isobel's home, paying his attentions to Mary. Alexander had one son, Aemilius, born in 1792 by his first wife, and two more by Mary — Thomas in 1808 and Alexander in 1811. George was to bring all three into the fur trade, and all played important roles in the life of the governor.

Alexander the schoolmaster was much more to the Simpson household, and especially to young George, than merely the schoolmaster. And he was more to the life of the town. He served as baillie of the burgh, commissioner of the Kirk Sessions, and leader of the men in hunts and excursions. George was an excellent horseman and shot with both rifle and pistol, skills fostered while in Dingwall.

Just what subjects were taught in the Dingwall school are not entirely clear. The usual subjects were English, writing, and arithmetic. Beyond those the teacher was given wide scope. Teachers in nearby parishes taught French language, geography, geometry, bookkeeping, different branches of practical mathematics, music, and so on. The optional subjects could vary considerably. What subjects beyond the usual George studied is unknown.

Cousin Alexander tells us that when George went to London in 1808 he was "clever, active, plausible, and full of animal spirits." As the seeds of the man are in the boy, these qualities must have been in the young George — likeable, friendly, active, intelligent … and tough. It's unlikely that any boy who challenged Simpson to a schoolyard fight came away unscathed. Alexander later claimed that "[Dingwall] school-fellows were bold and expert swimmers." George must have been one of those, as later in life he considered himself a champion swimmer, claiming "few can overmatch me in the water."

The Highlands are prized for trekking and hill-climbing today, as they were in Simpson's day. George's cousins, Thomas and Alexander, later spoke of "the sports and exercises of that wild and remote highland district," as they trekked the mountains together as summer exercise. Many opportunities exist near Dingwall to tax the energies of the intrepid climber. Hills surround Dingwall, and beyond looms the whale-back of Ben Wyvis, nine miles northwest of Dingwall, rising to 3,432 feet. George must have climbed this and other mountains, as later he could compare the heather of Scotland's mountaintops with that found in the Rocky Mountains of Canada.

Before leaving his schooling, we might consider what education Simpson did *not* get in Dingwall. There was nothing that might be called learning in a higher sense. This lack of sophistication was to serve Simpson well, as it helped to make him a plain-spoken man, without airs and graces. In this he was as one with the men of the Northwest, those straightforward fur-trade factors and traders with whom Simpson later worked. Distinguished historian E.E. Rich makes the astute point that much of Simpson's success in the leadership of men lay exactly here:

> There was little of the high flown idealist about George Simpson. His lack of airs probably goes as far to explain his success as do his determination

and vision. Certainly he shared to the full the ordinary life and pleasures among whom he worked; his creature comforts mattered to him, his enjoyment of them put him on the same level as the other fur traders.

These traits, then — the handwriting, the bookkeeping, the suavity of manners instilled by his grandmother, the friendliness of manner of the father, the steady intelligence and physical health of the mother — were all well-suited to the future success of George Simpson.

As his energies, intelligence, and abilities became evident as he grew out of childhood, George's family may have decided that he should join his uncles in London. It was commonplace in the mercantile world to take relatives into apprenticeships. Judging from our later knowledge, George's handwriting was distinct, his arithmetic exact, his mind precise and clear. He was taller than average, with a fine athletic build, and was in the bloom of health. He was personable and agreeable and handsome, with fine features, a head of wavy red hair, and intense blue eyes. His energies were indefatigable.

In 1808, Simpson, aged about sixteen, left for London. He likely travelled by the London smack, a coastal sailing ship that left from Dingwall each month for the capital, making the run in about four days.

We may imagine Simpson's first voyage, along the east coast of Scotland and England, turning into the Thames Estuary, the gradual filling of the channel with shipping, the appearance of sturdy English houses along the shore, the great shipping docks along the Thames, the masts of hundreds of ships piercing the horizon. Then, rising ominously on his right, the Tower of London, and just beyond it the vast, ornate Custom House with its crowds of ships, sea captains, customs officers, rumbling lorries, and labourers of all sorts.

Across Thames Street, a short walk up Dunstan Hill brings the traveller to the tall-spired church of St. Dunstan in the East, where the Simpsons worshipped. A few steps farther, the narrow street opens onto the broad avenue of Great Tower Street. Across the street, at the corner of Great Tower and Mincing Lane, stood the offices and residence of George's uncle, Geddes Mackenzie Simpson. There George would live and work for the next twelve years.

The High Street of Dingwall in the nineteenth century, much as George Simpson would have known it.

2

London: This Youth Is Just Come from the Highlands

In the end ... it will always pay to be fortunate in one's friends.
— Harold Clunn

While in London, Simpson lived in the part of the City immediately west of the Tower of London, called Tower Ward. The main thoroughfare there, Great Tower Street, ran at a diagonal, northwest from the tower. The third street branching from it on the north side was Mincing Lane, and it was on that corner that Simpson lived and worked, at 73 Great Tower Street. Because ocean-going vessels could not pass beyond London Bridge, ships were crowded along the Ward's riverbank and served by a vast ornate Custom House. For this reason, the Ward was crammed with dozens of businesses doing an overseas trade. Uncle Geddes's sugar supply company was one of those. So was the Hudson's Bay Company.

In those days, Tower Ward was full of "stinking Allies, dark, gloomy Courts and suffocating yards," all teeming with, "brutal, insolent and quarrelsome" labourers, where "pickpockets ... make no scruple to knock people down with bludgeons."

Mincing Lane, "like any minor street, was a close, dank thoroughfare, paved with cobblestones and strewn with straw, food, and feces; the smell of burning coal and the deafening noise of coaches, carts, horses, and dogs pushing their way through the slop was often overwhelming, even to the hardiest citizen."

The Custom House on the riverside below Great Tower Street unloaded wares from around the world. According to Nicholas Garry, the customs officers were "uncivil and intolerant," and "extraordinarily clever at finding anything contraband, a share going into their own pockets." The river filled with an astonishing number of ships, the wharves and streets teemed with sailors from around the world — rough, tough, and often drunk. The bargemen, complained one visitor, "use singular and even quite extraordinary terms, and generally very coarse and dirty ones, and I cannot explain them to you." Inside the Custom House, "the hall on the first floor was so crowded with merchants, captains of vessels, and other applicants that you have difficulty in making your way in."

Next to the Custom House stood Billingsgate Fish Market, where the "smell of whelkins, red-herrings, sprats, and a hundred other sorts of fish [was] almost unbearable." Here, a billingsgate — "a scolding, impudent slut" — could serve up "a dish of billingsgate" — an outpouring of the coarsest obscenities in London. Business was carried on in a half-drunken state. Beer, porter, ale, and gin were the drinks of the working classes, while the wealthier consumed quantities of port and Bordeaux claret.

It was in this beehive of roiling energy and activity that Simpson spent the next twelve years, a period vital for his future as governor of the HBC.

The building at 73 Great Tower Street contained business space on the ground floor and living quarters on the second. Apprentices like George slept in the attic. Geddes — "a nice-looking old man," a visitor later said — had married in 1805 and was starting a family, which eventually grew to fifteen children. His wife, Frances, "is a very pleasant-looking woman," said the same visitor, "and it is melancholy to see her, she is nothing but a *clocking* hen running after her family to make them take care of themselves." Letitia Hargrave, the visitor who saw them in 1840, called them all "delicate" with "a sort of simplicity."

In 1808, when George arrived, the business was run by Geddes and his partner, John Scott. Scott's son William — "a great fat good-humoured man" — was also beginning his apprenticeship that year and became a lifelong friend of George's. Also living nearby were three brothers of Geddes — Duncan, John, and Thomas — all described as sugar brokers.

There were others in this family group who were of higher social standing. There was, for instance, James Webster, who had a mansion in West Ham and another in Scotland. James Graham, in partnership with Geddes Simpson and after whom Geddes named a daughter, was his son. Family friend Sir Augustus D'Este was the grandson of George the Third, after whom George would name a daughter. And then there was Andrew Wedderburn —who would change his name to Andrew Colvile in 1812— from the great mercantile house of Wedderburn, who was to take Simpson under his wing and foster his career.

Thomas Douglas, the Fifth Earl of Selkirk, a major stockholder in the HBC, was quite familiar with the character of the young clerk. In the course of time, both he and Wedderburn were to press for Simpson's advancement in the HBC.

George Simpson was apprenticed as a mercantile broker, a period of training usually lasting seven years. Overseas brokering was a hazardous corner of merchandizing, involving the transfer of goods across the seven seas. "A London counting house," we are told, "was a commercial beehive, active, ordered, and integrated." Business was being conducted in the partners' rooms, the clerks besieged with public requests and orders. The training was close to drudgery — "painstaking copying of letters, endless repetition of tables of exchange, and attendance at some of the busiest concourses in London — all could sap the enthusiasm of the keenest apprentice."

The day ran from 9:00 a.m. until 2:00 p.m. and from 4:00 to 8:00 p.m., six days per week, with two afternoons off. The typical clerks' room contained a six-foot-long double desk, a merchant's bureau, a painted bookcase, and two chairs. On the walls were maps of the world and tables of international currency exchange. The bureau was neatly divided into compartments containing the necessary printed forms — London Dock Accounts, Custom House Duties, Contracts, Remittances, Average Documents, and Bills of Lading. George would have had to master these. The bookcase contained books on the trade, and these were expected to be read and understood. Because he did business with the HBC, Geddes's library would have been stocked with books on the North American fur trade. Simpson would have been expected to read these.

Great emphasis was placed on neatness. Each document was to be properly filed, and every clerk was expected to clear his own desk at the end of each day's work. An orderly clerks' room was an essential of business, and orderliness and efficiency were expected of the new apprentices.

As nothing could be left to chance, guesswork, or interpretation, it was necessary to spell out exactly what had to be done — what to do, when to do it, how to do it, who to do it — and this made necessary the mastering of the competent business letter, the ordinary means of communication between the businesses involved. The handwriting needed to be clear and legible and to the point, and the "spinning out of the long letter" became a required skill.

In all this there was an air of secrecy. In such a cut-throat trade, nothing to do with the business or the private lives of the traders could be divulged to competitors. In 1840, Letitia Hargrave complained, "they are all so wrapt up in mystery that I am afraid to say anything about the Company."

Communication in the city was immediate and oral, and it would have been George's duty to run errands, deliver copies, deal with officials in the Custom House, and carry instructions to the sea captains. All this would have taken George out of the counting house, into the streets and onto the docks of the city. Precision and politeness combined with friendliness and good communication skills would have been a necessity.

The warehouses were on the riverfront wharves and West India docks. When a ship arrived, the whole office staff would be there supervising the unlading, comparing the manifests with the actual goods, and seeing to the safe storage of the cargo. This, when he had advanced to the position of managing clerk, would have fallen under the supervisory duties of George Simpson. The men who actually did the labour would be ordinary workmen, those illiterate, rough Londoners who began their day with a pint of bitter and fortified themselves throughout the day with more of the same. It's more than likely that these men from time to time became cantankerous and insubordinate. Later, in Rupert's Land, Simpson became notorious for "knocking heads" to gain obedience, and it's entirely possible that he served his apprenticeship in this activity on the wharves of London.

It is one of the curiosities of this story that almost as soon as he arrived in London, young George Simpson found himself in the company of the three great tacticians who were to influence the fur trade for the next half-century: Sir Alexander Mackenzie, Andrew Wedderburn, and Thomas Douglas, Fifth Earl of Selkirk.

Soon after sixteen-year-old George arrived in London in 1808, he would have met his fourteen-year-old cousin, Geddes Mackenzie, from 12 Great Tower Street. She was the daughter of George Mackenzie, Second Laird Avoch and son of Captain John Mackenzie, First Laird Avoch, half-brother to George's grandmother, Isobel Mackenzie. This tangled web of family relationships became even stranger in 1812 when the seventeen-year-old Geddes Mackenzie married the fifty-year-old Sir Alexander Mackenzie. In this curious way, the great explorer became the cousin by marriage of the future governor.

Geddes and Alexander socialized extensively, holding Highland balls for London associates and friends from the north, to which Simpson, as cousin, Highlander, relative, and convivial spirit, would have been invited.

If there is one book we can be sure Simpson read, it is Sir Alexander Mackenzie's *Voyages from Montreal: On the River*

St. Lawrence, Through the Continent of North America, to the Frozen and Pacific Oceans, in the Years 1789 and 1793. With a Preliminary Account of the Rise, Progress, and Present State of the Fur Trade in That Country, Illustrated with Maps. Even the title is enough to whet the appetite for adventure, and the likelihood is that Simpson not only read the book, but discussed its contents with the author himself.

Voyages is not only a tale of adventure and discovery. It presents to the world ideas that Mackenzie was to "preach in season and out of season to all who would listen." He proposed no less than a giant monopoly straddling the land from the Canadas to the Pacific. Mackenzie's visionary plan was the first that advocated a united British presence from coast to coast, and as such can be considered the first presentation of a concept of nationhood under the British flag straddling the northern half of North America. George Simpson was there to hear it and discuss it with the great explorer.

When George Simpson arrived in London he met Andrew Wedderburn, now Andrew Colvile, a family friend of Geddes Mackenzie. Although Andrew was a half-generation older than George, they developed a friendship that lasted the rest of their lives. He was to become Simpson's benefactor, and the man chiefly responsible for his promotion to the North American governorship of the HBC.

In 1812, Colvile joined in business with the firm of Simpson and Graham and became George's employer. He took the energetic and efficient young apprentice under his wing. By 1815, George was Andrew's personal secretary, assisting him with his HBC duties. So George was not only getting the best business training, but was learning by personal contact the workings of the HBC.

Thomas Douglas was the brother-in-law of Andrew Colvile, and both had begun to buy up HBC stock with the intent of gaining control of the Company. But while Colvile's motives were profit, Selkirk's were humanitarian. His purpose was to begin a settlement in Rupert's Land at the confluence of the Red and Assiniboine rivers (modern Winnipeg). That settlement, he felt, could not only feed the settlers, but also provide much-needed supplies for the HBC.

However innocent of purpose, the Nor'westers did not appreciate Selkirk's plan to establish a food-producing colony on their line of communication from Montreal to the Athabasca. The NWC declared virtual war on the colony. Fields of grain were trampled, men and women were driven from their homes, some were carried off for resettlement in Canada, and in 1816 Governor Semple and twenty of his men were shot to death at Seven Oaks, just north of the settlement. Selkirk's thoughts of a peaceful outcome were dashed by the conflict between the two companies, which lasted until the union in 1821.

And where was George Simpson in the decade while all this was going on? He was in the clerk's room at the counting house, at the partner's table for meals, at the drawing room social events, listening to Andrew Colvile and Thomas Douglas expound on their ideas for transforming Rupert's Land. At other times he was in the drawing rooms of Sir Alexander Mackenzie, listening to the old adventurer propound his idea for a transcontinental empire of the fur trade. In this strange way the young apprentice was immersed in the ideas of both houses. In time it would be George Simpson's task to bring together the ideas of these three visionary men, as he sought to bring order out of chaos in the wreckage of the fur trade.

* * *

As the teens of the nineteenth century progressed, so did George's business fortunes. Even his two worst enemies admit as much. His cousin Alexander Simpson tells us that, once in London, "his advance was rapid, for he was clever, active, plausible, and full of animal spirits." Similarly, John MacLean said that by 1820, at the age of twenty-seven or twenty-eight, "his talents had advanced him to a seat at the first desk." We have no reason to doubt that his rise was rapid and that by 1820 he was the head clerk, a position, judging by his performance in the Athabasca a few months later, woefully inadequate for his abilities. By 1820 his place in the bland world of colonial brokerage seemed secure.

Historian E.E. Rich claims that when Simpson entered the fur trade in 1820, he was an "utter novice" and "complete greenhorn." But Simpson was no greenhorn, no novice. He had been in the company of Andrew Colvile since 1808 and had helped him in his capacity as Committee member. He knew personally the Earl of Selkirk and the other members of the Committee, and knew their tactical plans for victory in the Athabasca. He also knew Sir Alexander Mackenzie, with his breadth of knowledge of the Northwest and his geopolitical theory for a unified fur trade. As Simpson's responsibilities in the HBC grew, he was to gain increasing intimacy and understanding of the workings of the Company. When he entered Rupert's Land in 1820 he was a seasoned manager of men, expert bookkeeper and analytical accountant, and, behind it all, he had formed a concept for transcontinental mastery.

Just what kind of man Simpson was when he joined the HBC can be seen in a description of him written shortly after he joined the Company, by Colin Robertson, who Simpson had replaced in the Athabasca. It is a highly informative commentary:

There is an ease with which all evils are to be remedied.... He seems to have the whole business at his finger ends. I fear he deals too much in figures, for by one stroke of the pen he places a thousand bags of pemican *there*, so many hundreds of bushels of wheat at another place, and as for boats and canoes he sends them a-swimming while the bark is on the trees and the timber in the woods.... Now it never struck this gentleman, the impossibility of raising timber in a frozen swamp, when I mentioned this circumstance to Mr. Simpson the answer was, "Mr. McTavish informs me there is plenty of timber already raised." However, he is one of the most pleasant little men I have ever met with, full of spirits, can see no difficulties, and is ambition itself, and if he has a fault, he requires more the bridle than the spur.

Robertson was looking at greatness and could not understand it. Simpson's ease of command, the firm decision, the finger on the pulse, the refusal to see difficulties, the universal grasp of the task, and even the pleasing, friendly manner — all Robertson saw, but he saw them as flaws rather than virtues. Still, putting aside Robertson's failure of vision, his early description of Simpson caught the essence of the man, and remains one of the best ever written.

Another description was written twelve years after Simpson's death by Malcolm McLeod, the son of a fur-trade factor, who knew Simpson personally. He stresses the physical side of Simpson:

The late Sir George Simpson was, though not
tall, say about five feet seven at most,* of rather
imposing mien, stout, well-knit frame, and of
great expanse and fullness of chest, and with an
eye brightly blue, and ever a blaze in peace or
war, and with an address which ever combined
the *suaviter in modo, et fortiter in imperio* – [mild
in manner, bold in command.] His was, indeed
… an address to strike awe on his hearers.

Courage, ability, stamina, presence, and friendliness of
manner, combined with an enduring love of travel — these were
the qualities that brought success to George Simpson and great
esteem to the Honourable Hudson's Bay Company.

By 1820, Simpson was a finished gentleman moving com-
fortably among successful businessmen, Company share-
holders, and members of royalty and the peerage. He was a
man with abilities far beyond the needs of a sugar brokerage,
with, after twelve years, a close knowledge of the working of
the HBC. It would not have escaped the shrewd mind of the
young clerk that the lack of orderly arrangements was the root
cause of the disorder and lack of profits for the Company. And
it must have crossed his mind that the wilds of the Indian
Country were tailor-made to fulfill the sense of daring and
adventure that was part of his nature.

Several critical changes were taking place in the fur trade and
Simpson, as confidant of Andrew Colvile, would have known of
them. Lord Bathurst, Colonial Secretary, was becoming increas-
ingly concerned about the violence in the Northwest, and now

* The average height of men of his day was about five-feet, six-inches, so George Simpson was slightly
taller than most of the men of his time.

was on the verge of issuing a written directive to keep the peace. Like it or not, the war between the HBC and the NWC was about to end one way or another.

By 1820 the NWC was having second thoughts about its policy of violence, with company officers split on the effectiveness of the "gains of systematic villainy," as Simpson was later to put it. Word was out, as Colin Robertson reported, that "the winterers ... wanted œconomy in place of wanton expenditure and were convinced that no good had been derived from the violent measures."

The HBC was also having difficulty recruiting an effective governor. Governor Semple had been killed in 1816. It had tried to recruit Thomas Thomas, Governor of the Southern Department, but he had been reluctant to accept. It had tried Chief Factor James Bird, who had taken a temporary appointment "with reluctance" and showed "lack of decision." It had looked outside its own officers but negotiations had gone nowhere. Finally, almost in desperation, it had appointed William Williams, ship's captain in the service of the East India Company, known for his strict discipline.

However, in 1819 Governor Williams had rashly arrested a number of NWC officers, all done with a dubious legality. Now a bench warrant was out for Williams. If he were arrested and off the scene, HBC interests would be without leadership in North America. On short notice it had to find a temporary replacement. It could be said that the HBC turned to Simpson as a last resort.

The appointment of George Simpson as shadow governor-in-chief to William Williams in North America was perhaps the shrewdest appointment the HBC ever made. Simpson's commission was a power and authority in potential rather than real fact, to become effective if an attempt should be made "to drag Governor

Williams out of the Country," or Simpson's assistance was deemed "of essential importance." It wasn't much, but Simpson was about to make the most of it.

In late February 1820, Simpson was introduced to the HBC Committee. He then departed London for Liverpool, where he boarded the ship *James Monroe* bound for New York City, arriving there on April 4.

From there he passed swiftly to Montreal, where he arrived on April 28, and where he was feted by local dignitaries. Then he left via the Ottawa River and Lakes Huron and Superior by express canoe for the interior. He stopped at Fort William (modern Thunder Bay, Ontario) on May 28, where he daringly entered the enemy camp to deliver Lord Bathurst's letter and "the North West saw for the first time one of the most remarkable men in the history of Rupert's Land."

By early July he had arrived at Norway House, where he learned that Governor Williams had escaped arrest and would be in charge for the winter campaign. But Williams had something else to offer Simpson. Colin Robertson, the man in charge of the Athabasca District, had been captured on June 29 and taken to the Canadas for trial, and would not be available to take charge of his district that winter. Would Simpson be good enough to take command of the Athabasca campaign? Simpson "readily assented."

George Simpson was not to be acting governor that winter, but that was just as well. Governor Williams would sit far from the action, unable to influence the course of events about to unfold in the Athabasca. But Simpson, as factor in charge of the Athabasca, would be in the thick of the fray, leading the campaign, learning the trade in an ordeal of fire — and incidentally proving his mettle to the Governor and Committee in London.

It was the cast of the die for him in Rupert's Land. By July 30, 1820, he was taking his departure for the interior. It had all happened so quickly, and to the twenty-eight-year-old George it seemed like a boy's adventure. "I am armed to the Teeth," he wrote, and "will sell my Life if in danger as dear as possible, and never allow a North Wester [to] come within reach of my Riffle if Flint Steel and Bullet can keep him off."

3

Rupert's Land: War in the Athabasca

Few ... have ever seized Fortune ... with more
briskness and audacity.
                                    — Chester Martin

*Portrait of George Simpson
circa 1820, about the time he
entered the fur trade.*

When Simpson was appointed factor-in-chief of the Athabasca District in the summer of 1820, those hardened old fur traders had good reason to express their doubts about this dapper man going into the Northwest dressed in his London business suit and accompanied by a pet terrier named Boxer. Many of the old Nor'westers, and Bay men as well, would probably have agreed with Norwest fur trader W.F. Wentzell when he said "Mr. Simpson, a gentleman from England, superintends their business. His being a strange, and reputedly gentlemanly, man, will not create much alarm, nor do I presume him formidable as an Indian trader."

Moreover, declared Wenzell, whose claim to a footnote in history now rests on his misjudgment of George Simpson:

> The NWC in Athabasca has been so liberally supplied with men and goods that it will be almost wonderful if the opposition can make good a subsistence during the winter. Fort Chipewyan alone has an equipment of no less than seventy men, enough to crush their rivals.

But Simpson's worst enemy may not have been the Nor'westers. Simpson soon discovered that his efforts were being sabotaged by men of the HBC. The culprit was fellow officer John Clarke, who, Simpson complained later, "appropriated the Flower of the people, and a great many more than the Governor intended, endeavoured to incite the Canadians against me … monopolized property of every description intended for the use of the Athabasca, and made over the refuse of Men and Goods to me." There were men within the Company, apparently, who would have secretly rejoiced to see Simpson chewed up in the Athabasca.

When, on July 30, 1820, Simpson opened a new logbook to begin his *Journal of Occurrences*, he is in command from the first words:

> Governor Williams, having been pleased to invest me with the charge of the Athabasca [Department] in the absence of Mr. Robertson, I have abandoned my intention of returning to England this season, in the hope that my presence in the Interior may be of some advantage to the Company's affairs in that quarter, and I intend that the following Journal shall give an accurate and unbiased report of the principal Occurrences that may take place within my observation.

Simpson left Norway House for the Athabasca leading a brigade of "twelve canoes navigated by sixty-eight men, containing two hundred and fifty-four pieces, which I suspect is far short of what the Department requires, we must however make the most of everything." For a journey of nearly a thousand miles, the canoes were in a "very crazy state," and for days he could not leave Norway House because "the Guides and men [were] in a state of inebriety," having bartered their shirts and blankets for rum.

Simpson's journey to the North was characterized by the speed that would become his trademark. But it was not speed against caution. These were still dangerous times, and Simpson was not to be ambushed at the Grand Rapids, where the Saskatchewan River enters Lake Winnipeg: "We have therefore provided our people with a musket and bayonet each and ten rounds of ball cartridge, and armed ourselves for the purpose of

Self defence." As an extra precaution, he continued, they "sent two men across the Portage to reconnoiter ... arranged our arms, and sat up all night, as we suspected the N.W. Halfbreeds were laying in ambush for us."

No ambush being set, no Nor'westers in sight, Simpson proceeded on a "hard days march," and that night they slept on the banks of the river in flood, and "actually floated in our blankets, and were tormented by Myriad of Moschetos."

The team sped forward, passing a NWC brigade, and Simpson could not help remarking that "all their canoes are new and well built," while the HBC canoes were "old, crazy, and patched up" and manned by "old and infirm creatures or Porkeaters [new recruits] unfit for the arduous duty they have to perform.... There is much room for improvement."

On August 22, Simpson met Simon McGillivray of the NWC, and commented that McGillivray had "been most active in every nefarious transmission that has taken place in Athabasca, he is notorious for his low cunning ... he seems to have mistaken his trade as he possesses sufficient artifice to have ranked high as a tip staff in the civilized world." In the Athabasca that winter, McGillivray would be his most dangerous opponent.

Later, Simpson came up to an HBC brigade, using the occasion to pass "some encomiums on the Guides and men and for their activity," and to give "a dram to the people and a supper for the Officers and Guides." Simpson was all charm and goodwill. On finding a group of Natives, Simpson "made a speech and gave some Rum and Tobacco." He already knew how to make the strokes.

In speedy time, Simpson's brigade reached Cumberland House on the Saskatchewan. He had pushed his men hard: "We have made a holyday in order to recruit our people who are much fatigued."

On reaching the twelve-mile Methye Portage, the height of land between Hudson Bay and the Arctic, Simpson treated the men "with an extra dram, otherwise he is subject to the unpleasant process of shaving." And always eager to keep the goodwill of his voyageurs, he "indulged the people with a bottle of rum." Thus inspired, the brigade delivered Simpson to Fort Wedderburn in three days, where he arrived on September 20, 1820.

George Simpson was not pleased with what he found. "For various inexplicable causes," he jabbed at Williams, the *Govr. in Chief* [Simpson's emphasis], he found the fort "in fully as good a state as I had reason to expect," which was pretty bad:

> [The fort] had certainly a very desolate appearance … the business left in a most irregular state … the Stores empty, the people in a state of mutiny, and a congregation of evils staring in the face those in charge of the Company's affairs: the Indians were discontented, we had not a pound of ammunition to give them, the Fishery for a length of time was unsuccessful, no provisions on hand; in short, both our Indians and people were reduced by starvation to a miserable extent.

Having deftly excoriated Williams for his mismanagement, Simpson gives himself a pat on the back:

> The Brigade [which Simpson had just led into the Athabasca] was by all accounts as indifferently equipped as any that ever entered the North, yet it arrived within one day of the North West [Company brigade] and every package

was delivered in good condition.... The Canoes were in very bad repair.... I was really ashamed to see the miserable slovenly figure we made alongside our Opponents.... The Goods for the different posts were all packed up higledy pigledy at the Depot, the packages incorrectly marked and numbered, and the contents not corresponding to the Invoices, the consequence was that Mr. Miles had to open every individual package and select the goods *de novo* according to the Indents; this operation detained more than one hundred men here for eight days at a time when there were upwards of two hundred souls, men, women and children about the Fort, the people continually grumbling about their short allowance of provisions, the Indians tormenting us for liquor and their equipments, and the North West emissaries using every means to debauch them, in short the incessant clamour and uproar occasioned by these concurrent difficulties was truly vexacious.

Although Governor Williams had appointed the officers, Simpson now blandly informed him that "circumstances have induced me to make some trifling alterations in your arrangement of the Officers." He then proceeded to make widespread reappointments of his officers, reassigning the posts, demoting and promoting as necessary. He mollified those officers who had not received the posts they wanted. The post at St. Mary's on the Peace River was found to be "sadly mismanaged" during the summer, the officer instructed summarily "to deliver the charge" to Duncan

Finlayson. Interpreter Lalonde was reprimanded "on his intimacy with the people, cautioned him against indulging them too much." He severely lectured two of the people for "neglect of duty" during the summer, and one of them "inclined to be impertinent ... and hinted at joining the N.W., but when I talked hand-cuffs & short allowance he lowered his tone."

Great show was spent on the Natives, "to whom I have given a regale on the occasion of my arrival." A day later he "made a speech in great form to the Indians which seemed to give satisfaction; much of my time is occupied in conversing with these people; they look upon me as the greatest man ever to come into the country." Sometimes his interference went beyond mere business. When a Chipewyan woman proved unfaithful to her husband, Simpson "gave a private lecture to the Lady, threatening to transform her into a dog if she repeated the sin." Even this was good for business, as "with the assistance of this Oracle, I have wrought on their superstitious ideas as far as to persuade them that I can discover every skin that is privately sold to the N.W. Coy."

The posts were spread for hundreds of miles to the north along the Slave and Mackenzie rivers, south along the Athabasca and Clearwater, and west along the Peace River. He could not visit them all. He would have to resort to another of his secret weapons — the letter. Each weakness in the post officers was noted, each admonished with deft skill. One was advised to discontinue "the extravagant system which had hitherto been pursued" and to adopt œconomy. Others were told to avoid "jealousies and private misunderstandings" with fellow officers. With another, Simpson trusted that the rumour of the officer "being rather addicted to the Bottle" was untrue and urged sobriety. Finlayson was praised for seeing eye to eye with Simpson on the matter of "an Œconomical system." Those dissatisfied with their salaries were offered a higher rate if they signed for three years. Hurt egos were stroked. To all, Simpson gave a few official hints: "Œconomy must now be the order of the day.... Œconomy must be studied with unremitting attention.... I have to entreat that you study œconomy.... Beaver is the sole object of our mission.... It is by the number of Packs alone that the ... [HBC] can appreciate the Talents of their Traders.... Impress on the minds of the Indians that the Company is rich, powerful, and strictly honorable and that our Opponents are the reverse."

On one day, when Simpson found that the "people are inclined to be mutinous," he complained, "I must however at present submit to their misconduct and endeavour to coax them into good humour." But three days later, when "one of the men, a ringleader, absolutely refused to embark and foreseeing the dangerous consequences of permitting such flagrant misconduct to pass unnoticed, I gave Mr. Miles the hint, who enforced the order with very little ceremony by giving the fellow a shaking he is not likely to forget and dragging him into his Canoe, where he found it necessary to do his duty without further hesitation."

And so it went as economy and order were established in his district, with Simpson masterminding the whole with an adroit hand.

Meanwhile, the war in the Athabasca was about to heat up. Simpson found that "the No[rth] West have as usual been most insolent, they have repeatedly threatened to take the Fort and people, and frequently paraded in front of our Gates exhibiting their swords & pistols." But Simpson was already taking counter-measures. With the Nor'westers erecting a watch house near the gate of the fort, Simpson noted: "I intend erecting a similar building close to their Stockades." His officers were advised against the "inveterate machinations of our Opponents," and instructed to "protect the lives of yourself and people ... by every means *however desperate* within your power."

With the onset of winter in 1820, the long-awaited clash was about to occur in three dangerous skirmishes between October 19 and 23.

In early October, McGillivray and his bullies had occupied the NWC watch house, which stood a few feet from the HBC bastion and jutted out some fifteen feet beyond: "from their back windows they command a full view of all our proceedings, which is extremely unpleasant." Simpson sent a work party out to erect a stockade extending from the fort, toward the lake, and by this means obscure their view. McGillivray, "in a peremptory tone," ordered the men to stop. On hearing this, Simpson "called the Gentlemen together, also three or four most confidential men ... then proceeded to the spot ... and directed the workmen to go on with their business." McGillivray and his men responded, with each "a dirk and a brace of large pistols, not fastened as usual in their belts, but held openly to view in their hands." Simpson reported the ensuing conversation verbatim:

> "My name is Simpson, I presume yours is McGillivray." [H]e replied: "It is." — I then said, "I intend erecting these Stockades from the corner of the Bastion in a direct line to that stump" (pointing to the stump of a Tree, about five feet within another stump which is understood to be the boundary of the two establishments). "Pray Sir, what are your objections?" He answered: "I understand from Mr.

Oxley that he intended to run them beyond the boundary line which I shall not permit." I rejoined: "we have no intention to encroach on what is understood to be the line of demarkation, nor shall we tamely submit to any encroachment on our rights, we are inclined to be quite orderly neighbors if permitted to be so, but are determined to maintain our privileges with firmness, and shall promptly resent any injury or insult that may be offered." He sullenly replied: "time will show."

At this point, Simpson added:

[I]n the interim, my Tarrier Dog Boxer (a very playful fellow) was amusing himself with a stick ... and while the Bully was regarding him with an ill-natured look, as if about to give him a kick, I with a smile addressed the dog: "come here, Boxer, you do not seem to be aware that you are committing a trespass." McGillivray, with a good deal of asperity, observed: "We have no intention to molest your dog, Sir," to which I replied: "Nor shall you his Master with impunity."

It was a tricky standoff, and McGillivray and his bullies "retired somewhat crestfallen, and in the course of two hours afterwards, the fence was completed and an annoyance removed."

The score was one for Simpson, zero for the NWC.

But McGillivray was not to be so easily beaten. A few days later, one of Simpson's workmen, a man named Taylor, came in to say that while he had been carrying wood near the NWC stockade, he had been set upon by two bullies, who knocked him to the ground. They "beat and kicked him in a most inhuman manner … he permitted the poor fellow to crawl away detaining his cap and fire wood as a trophy of Victory." Once more, Simpson "put his Gentlemen under arms, manned the Bastion, and directed Taylor and another man to go for the wood that was taken from him and authorised the man who accompanied him to shoot any person who interfered with them, and that we should protect them."

The wood and cap were returned without incident, other than Simpson gave McGillivray "a solemn warning never to assault, interfere with, or insult any person connected with the Honble. [HBC], as I was determined to protect them whatever might be the consequences."

Simpson was ahead two to zero.

The next day, McGillivray tried again, this time attempting to erect a bastion "encroaching about three feet within the line that was acknowledged by Mr. McGillivray on the 19th inst. to be the boundary of the two establishments." Simpson made the most of the moment: "[My officers] unanimously agreed to act in strict obedience to my directions: arms and ammunition were brought into the Hall, and I shewed the example by loading my double barrel'd gun and pistols with Ball."

Then it was out to the fray, but not before Simpson armed himself with one more weapon in his armoury. As it turned out, Simpson had an ace up his sleeve. Professing to know nothing about it until that moment, he found that a certain Mr. Grignon, a clerk in his employ, held a warrant for the arrest of Simon McGillivray. Simpson informed Grignon that if he wished to arrest Mr. McGillivray "in his Official capacity of a Constable," and if they were "Legally called upon for protection or assistance, [they would have] no alternative" but to assist. And so poor Grignon, cajoled into asking for assistance "in the Kings-name," with warrant in hand, was marched out to face the heavily armed McGillivray and his bullies. Simpson, "having shewed the example by loading my double barrel'd gun and pistols with Ball" and surrounded by three officers, a dozen men, and Grignon, marched to the bastion:

> Mr. McGillivray and several people armed immediately joined us, he came up to the spot where I stood with his hand on the hilt of his Dagger, and when close to each other I said, "Mr. McGillivray, I should be glad to have some further conversation with you on the subject of this boundary line." [H]e was about to reply when Mr. Grignon collared him and said "I arrest you in the Kings name." [H]e made some resistance and the Officer called out, "I demand your assistance in the Kings name," on which two of our people rushed upon the prisoner, disarmed him, and conveyed him into Fort Wedderburne.

The war was over. The rest was comic relief. The bullies scattered in confusion. One made "a precipitate retreat," another showed "an active pair of heels," another "took refuge in the woods," reported a straight-faced Simpson.

A few minutes later, Simpson sat at his desk as if nothing had happened, listening to McGillivray "venting his spleen in a torrent of abuse." Simpson simply responded that he had had nothing to do with it, that "the Officer had acted on his own responsibility and could alone be liable for the consequences." Then Simpson turned to his desk and went on with the business of the Company — and incidentally set an "Officer and three men with Bayonets and loaded Musquets [to] stand sentry every night," to prevent any attempt to rescue his prisoner.

It was three for Simpson, zero for the Nor'westers.

Of course, this was not the end of the story. The NWC built its bastion, now well on its own side of the line, and Simpson built his counter-bastion. McGillivray escaped a month later. But the wind was knocked out of the NWC. By December, so roundly had the tables been turned that when the opposition officer-in-charge, George Keith, sent an "impertinent note ... relative to a dog we claim," Simpson let it be known that he was "determined on seizing or shooting some of the N.W. Dogs ... in the proportion of 6 to 1." Three days later Simpson could report: "Mr. Keith ... has been pleased to give directions for the delivery of the dog we claim."

The war in the Athabasca had fizzled out in a farce.

Simpson could now turn his attention to tightening his grip on his authority. Officers who had not yet learned the art of writing reports were wryly reminded of their duty. Duncan Finlayson, who in time would become one of Simpson's closest allies, was told that his "dispatch consists of a small sized piece of Post widely penned and a margin of about an inch." Finlayson's next report was a "full, particular, and interesting communication," which was "very satisfactory" to Simpson. Similarly, he wrote to W.S. McBean at Colvile House, thanking him for the "pleasure of receiving your laconic communication of 27 [October]; my previous request seems to have escaped your recollection or been misunderstood, as instead of a full and particular statement of every thing worthy of remark, you have favoured me with a brief hurried note on a quarter sheet of paper." That was enough to correct the omission, and soon Simpson was receiving reports that permitted him to make arrangements of posts for the coming year.

He let one officer know that he would "have cause to repent the neglect of duty." To another he let know that his orders were "not to be disputed." When Jonas Oxley, an ex-army officer who felt himself hard done by, demanded satisfaction — "The injuries you have been so active to esteablish [Simpson quotes the letter with all its warts] against my character claiems an explenation & Satisfaction both to my Honour & the ranke I hold in his Majisty's servis," — Simpson shot back:

> Your impertinent and ridiculous note ... shall
> be treated with the sovereign contempt it merits.
> Your Honor and rank in his Majesty's Service
> are quite immaterial to me and all I require of
> you is to do your duty faithfully as a Clerk of the
> Honorable Hudson's Bay [Company].

Oxley was sent to the fisheries to fend for himself, where he continued to grumble; in the spring, Simpson took him out of the Athabasca and appropriately drummed him out of the Company's service.

Simpson proceeded to build a new Fort Wedderburn, stronger and better-equipped than before, ordered a stable built for the import of horses, established new fisheries, and, of course, built his bastion, which gave a fine outlook over NWC operations next door and "looked formidable."

When Simpson found that John Lee Lewes, officer in charge at Lesser Slave Lake, was not helping Duncan Finlayson on the Peace River, Simpson sent a letter that nicely admonished the man with a deft hand, while directing him to his duty:

> It is with much regret I learn from Mr. Finlayson that you have rendered him *NO* assistance, which has seriously injured our prospects in Peace River. It is possible that the Trade of Lesser Slave Lake and St. Mary's may occasionally interfere with each other and that trifling losses are sustained through the roguery of Indians and Freemen, but altho' you do belong to different Departments it should be recollected that we are all labouring in the same Vineyard, and that our utmost exertions should be united for the general interest … let me therefore entreat you that nothing like internal opposition should influence your conduct towards Mr. Finlayson, but that you render him every assistance in your power as I am satisfied that he will make no demands that he can possibly avoid.

While Simpson was at Fort Wedderburn, a British expedition to explore the north coast of North America was in progress. It was under the command of Captain John Franklin, whose expedition would meet with a tragic end in the ice twenty-five years later. Franklin was running short of supplies and sent his young midshipman, George Back, to Lake Athabasca to bring back extra stores. Back was arrogant, and did not hesitate to turn his requests into demands. George Simpson gave him a lesson he was never to forget.

When Back's demands were not immediately met, he wrote impertinently, reminding Simpson, "you have had several arrivals during my residence here and I imagine they were not all empty," to which Simpson snapped back, "The arrivals you allude to have no connection with the Goods expected from Isle ala Crosse and your conjecture that 'they were not empty' is perfectly just, but I presume you will give me leave to know the purpose for which they were intended."

George Back was to become in time Rear Admiral Sir George Back; in 1857 he praised the work of the HBC.

Except perhaps for Jonas Oxley and John Clarke, by spring Simpson could report that "a proper degree of subordination I am glad to find is at length gaining ground amongst the people all over the country."

With the end of winter and the trading season, Simpson turned his attention to praising his men for a job well done. To Ignace Giasson, who was considered lost on the west side of the mountains, Simpson expressed his "unspeakable satisfaction as from your non-arrival ... I was very apprehensive that some unfortunate accident had occurred to the party." To Vital Bourassa at Colvile House, Simpson expressed the opinion that "young Gentlemen of your zeal and activity must get forward in the service." George Andries is praised for the "zeal and interest" he had shown. To Mr. Greill, at Berens House, Simpson begged to express his "approbation of [his] conduct throughout the Winter."

When it appeared the very capable Duncan Finlayson was about to quit the country, Simpson turned on all his powers of persuasion to have him remain:

> Let me entreat that you will endeavour to alter your plans; the work of reform you have commenced would be accomplished in another year which would not fail of not only giving you much satisfaction but highly gratifying to the [Honourable] Committee who shall be informed to whom the merit is due.

Later, he wrote again to Finlayson with genuine sympathy at the hardships of the winter:

> I am really grieved at your sufferings and trust that you and the people are safe. Keep up your spirits, the good cheer at the Depot will efface the recollection of our miseries in Athabasca.... Let every Guide and man who can wield a paddle come out except those appointed to remain inland.

Such expressions of real concern and goodwill on Simpson's part could not have but touched the hearts of his officers, bucked up their will to survive and their desire to serve the Company well, and to return the good wishes to their governor who so deeply felt for and who had shared in their suffering. Few officers could have remained indisposed to their officer-in-chief after such heartfelt sympathies. He had shared their bitter winter, they had fought together their two implacable enemies — the elements and the NWC — and now they would share the cheer together at the depot.

Simpson's leadership was complete. He had seized power with an audacity that must have startled some and nonplussed others. But one thing was clear — no one would underestimate George Simpson again.

Simpson left the Athabasca on May 26, 1821, the lake and river still full of floating ice. But if Simpson wished a race against distance, the trip out would instead be a race against starvation. The supplies were meagre: "one bag pemmican, a little dried meat, a few geese, to do twenty men and four passengers for about nine days." As a consequence, the brigade had barely made it across Lake Athabasca when the men were described as "so much worn out by starvation that they are unable to make an expeditious journey." Only with the greatest difficulty did the men make it across the Methye Portage, so hungry they "began to exhibit fear of starvation."

On June 6, Simpson wrote that "our people are nearly worn out with hunger and fatigue, indeed myself and the other Gentlemen are in the same state, having had little or no sustenance for eleven days."

Driving relentlessly forward on empty stomachs was too much for the men. On June 7 they attempted to mutiny:

> Several of the people were extremely insolent,
> and refused to ship a small Box, one in partic-
> ular was so mutinous that I found it necessary
> to plunge into the Water, and drag him ashore

for the purpose of compelling him to embark the box.

Luckily, food was available at the next station, and for the first time in many weeks the men could indulge. But the start next day was delayed: "all our people very unwell in consequence of eating immoderately after their long fast."

On June 15 the brigade reached Cumberland House, where the men were rested while the canoes underwent repairs. On June 16 they "embarked at two o'clock a.m. The weather extremely hot and the flies very troublesome." On June 18 the Grand Rapids of the Saskatchewan were reached. Here Simpson gave himself a treat:

> Left our encampment at 4:00 a.m., landed Messrs. Miles and Oxley with two men out of each Canoe, as it is considered dangerous to run the Rapid with a full complement, and in six minutes got to the basin of the Upper Portage, a distance of about two miles: this is considered the finest run in North America, and altho' the swell is heavy it is by no means a dangerous rapid.

At the foot of the rapids the brigade heard of the coalition of the two companies. Simpson heard the news with an element of regret: "I must confess my own disappointment that instead of a junction our Opponents have not been driven out of the field, which with one or two years of good management I am certain might have been affected." With Simpson in charge, who could doubt it.

The next day Simpson arrived at Norway House, where he "was received with much politeness and attention by the Governor in Chief." But William Williams was not governor-in-chief anymore. On March 28, 1821, the London Committee had appointed two governors; Williams and Simpson were now equals in the trade.

At Rock Depot, Simpson completed his *Athabasca Journal and Report*. His general observations were scathing, not just to the officers who had previously fought the battle in the Athabasca, but also to the Committee, which had fostered the situation:

> It appears to me that the affairs of Athabasca have been hitherto totally neglected or sadly mismanaged, yet it affords me peculiar sat-isfaction to be enabled to state that generally speaking they begin to assume a more favour-able appearance, and if the advantages already gained, and so dearly bought, are followed up with system and regularity and that the neces-sary support is rendered in Men and Goods, I venture to predict that the Trade of the Department will in the course of Two or Three Years repay the heavy losses already sustained and thereafter prove a very lucrative concern. Had the management of the business been in competent hands, and conducted with ordinary discretion, it would long ere now have assumed a very different appearance, and the fatality which seems to have attended it been avoided;

but to mismanagement and the total absence of decision and salutary arrangement, more than the Opposition of the North West Compy. are to be imputed the misfortunes with which it would appear the concern has been haunted.

It was a stinging assessment of the futile years of conflict that had preceded his arrival.

Fort Chipewyan and Lake Athabasca. Watercolour by George Back, circa 1832.

When Simpson went into the Northwest in 1820, his authority had been outlined in the sketchiest terms, and in the course of the Athabasca campaign he chose to define his powers with a broad brush. He had mastered the NWC and the elements, imposed peace and order on a chaotic Athabasca District, and introduced a policy of economy and good management. Now, as he rode triumphant out of the Athabasca, he had mastered the

HBC itself. He had usurped Williams's governorship and, indeed, much of the governing powers of the HBC Committee in London — though none of them were quite aware of it yet — and he would not give them up for the rest of his life.

"It is one of the great coincidences of this story," marvelled historian Rich, "that, as the Company at last achieved mastery, it found in George Simpson its master."

4

Red River:
Recall Your Memory to That Summer

Now by flattery, now by firmness,
he bent men to his will.
— W. Stewart Wallace

In 1821 the NWC and the HBC joined together to form a new company under the name of the Hudson's Bay Company. The first question of business was this: who would be appointed governor of the Northern Department? Williams was the senior governor by one day, but the fact that Simpson had demonstrated superior management in the Athabasca forced the hand of all, and the governorship went to him.

And what a department! Nothing less than all of modern Canada, west of Hudson Bay, including the states of Washington and Oregon — a third of North America. All of this vast empire, for the first time in its history, was now a centralized regime under a single commander — George Simpson. His official title was that of governor; his honorific was His Excellency. However, with the enormous extent of territory and the diverse peoples he governed, his territory was soon likened to an empire, and in the course of time, Simpson was informally referred to as the "Scottish Emperor of the Fur Trade."

The burden of governance was immense. In 1670, King Charles of England had created, by charter, a colonial state and given governance of it to the Hudson's Bay Company. Its powers were similar to those of a modern state — sovereignty within its borders, exclusive rights to carry on its business, to make laws, and to enforce those laws. It was both a business and a government.

But the Northern Department lay in ruins after twenty-five years of opposition, the beaver depleted by over-trapping, the forts multiplied needlessly with the Union, its territory previously run by "numerous petty officers subject to no efficient control and practically answerable to none for abuse of power." At Red River the settlers, without laws to guide them, were in need of assistance. And across the mountains, the newly inherited Columbia District was a questionable enterprise, poorly managed and losing money, under siege on land and sea from American and Russian traders.

Simpson undertook the challenge with his usual ease, tackling the problems one at a time, travelling in ever-widening circles, which occupied his energies for the rest of the decade. But when he was finished, the department was a smoothly running operation, men and settlers alike happy.

When the old Nor'westers and the Bay men met in 1821 at York Factory for the first time after the union, an icy chillness existed between them after twenty years of battle. Old animosities were hard to forgive, and the two sides barely talked to each other. It was time for Simpson to turn on his charm. Many years after the event an admiring officer recalled the occasion:

> I would endeavour to recall your memory to the summer immediately succeeding the junction of the two companies, when that formidable band of Nor-West partners first landed on the bleak banks of York Factory, a bold energetic race of breached Highlanders from the North; the heroes of the opposition who had fought and bled manfully in that long contest now ended. They had undoubtedly been defeated in the struggle, and their very name as a body in the commercial world [was] now entirely defunct; yet they were by no means, apparently, humbled, or in the least subdued in spirit, but stalked about the buildings of the old dilapidated fort with the same haughty air and independent step as if they had merely met, as they were wont to do in the more successful times at their favourite depot Fort William.... At length the bell summoned us to dinner, when forthwith in walked the heterogeneous mass of human beings, but in perfect silence and with the most solemn gravity. As the whole group stood on the floor of that gigantic mess-hall, evidently uncertain how they would seat themselves at the table.... [They] would not amalgamate, for the Nor'westers in one compact body kept together and evidently had no inclination at first to mix up with their old rivals in trade. But that crafty fox

> ... George Simpson, coming hastily to the rescue
> with his usual tact and dexterity on such occa-
> sions, succeeded ... somewhat in dispelling that
> reserve in which both parties had hitherto con-
> tinued to envelope themselves.... It soon became
> evident that his stratagems in bows and smiles
> alone would eventually succeed in producing
> the desired effect on the exterior appearance of
> his haughty guests. Their previously stiffened
> features began to relax a little; they gradually but
> slowly mingled together, and a few of the better
> disposed, throwing themselves unreservedly in
> the midst of the opposite party, mutually shook
> each other by the hand. Then, and not till then,
> were they politely beckoned to their appointed
> places at the mess-table.

By the end of that first banquet Simpson had succeeded in turning the corner toward cordiality and co-operation.

Still, the first meeting of Council, in August 1821, was a fractious affair. To Colin Robertson, one of the Bay men, "it would appear ... that the North West Company had gained a complete victory and were dictating to us as to the terms of capitulation." On the surface that appeared to be the case: two-thirds of the appointments went to the Nor'westers. By the end of that first meeting, the Nor'westers could brag, "the governor is nobody now," and Robertson could complain that "the N.W.C. have gained a complete victory for the best places."

But the Nor'westers' victory would be short-lived. Simpson had a year to prove himself, and when Council met again in 1822, the balance of power had shifted into the hands of the governor.

At the second Council, Simpson quickly took control. He found that by "adopting calm and conciliatory measures generally and a little firmness when necessary they are to be managed." In the case of Colin Robertson, when Simpson found him "noisy" and "talked of rights and previledges ... in short wished to be a Leader ... I made such an exposure ... of his maladministration in the Saskatchewine and told him so many home truths in the presence of the whole Council that he is quite crestfallen and I think will give no more trouble." With the rest of the Council he "found it necessary to give them a lecture, which ... made them look on each other with suspicion and restored their confidence in myself."

The second Council resolved that "Governor Simpson be fully empowered to decide upon whatever steps he may consider necessary, both at this place and inland, from breaking up of this Council until the meeting of Council next year." From that moment on, Simpson was the supreme commander, whose will was to be obeyed.

And Wentzell, who had been so smug in 1820, wailed, "The northwest is beginning to be ruled with a rod of iron," and quit the service.

In the fall of 1821, Simpson undertook a grand tour of the Company forts along the Saskatchewan and Assiniboine rivers. With the Union, there were too many trading posts, too many men in the Company's employ. He would get to meet his officers and men, to let them see what kind of man he was, and to instill in them a sense of service to the Company.

Winter journeying must have been unusually thrilling for the new governor. Travel was by carriole — an enclosed sled, pulled by dogs "strongly resembling the wolf in size, and frequently in colour." The passengers were wrapped up in the carriole during travel, "the gently undulating motion of the sledge, in accommodating itself to the inequalities of the frozen surface ... strangely suggestive of the progress of a canoe over water faintly ruffled by a passing breeze." It was all very pleasant, but "to a strong man there is something humiliating being hauled about in a portable bed, like some feeble invalid, while the hardy voyageurs are maintaining their steady pace from hour to hour, day to day, week to week, for fatigue seems to them an unknown word."

George Simpson was not about to be hauled about in a portable bed. On the winter road he made it to Rock Depot in four and a half days — a new record. Getting out of his carriole, he learned to walk on snowshoes, and made Oxford House in three and half days — another record, of course. His penchant for travelling at speed for new records was now set, and would remain a feature of his governorship for the rest of his life.

At Norway House, Simpson and Colin Robertson took the measure of each other. Robertson found in Simpson "one of the most pleasant little men I have ever met with." For Simpson, Robertson was "a pleasant Gentlemanly Fellow.... As a man of business he does not shine, but has every inclination to conform to well-digested regulations." At each station he would have made similar judgments of each of his factors, traders, and clerks, down to the interpreters and assistants.

From Norway House he crossed Lake Winnipeg and travelled up a frozen Athabasca River to Cumberland House. His visit would have been announced, and his arrival expected, perhaps with some anticipation, and certainly with some trepidation. Lookouts would be stationed on the ramparts, and on Simpson's approach, rifles fired into the air to alert the factor and his men. What pomp and ceremony could be mustered at –22° Fahrenheit was performed — the greeting at the gate, the ceremonious entry into the fort — and the governor was welcomed into the spartan resources of the post.

Years after the events being described here, Frederick Graham, an English sporting gentleman, was appalled by the sight of a typical trading post:

> I hate the sight of these forts. Strange, large tumbledown places, like lumber rooms on a vast scale. All the white men living in them, look as if they had been buried for a century or two, and dug up again, and had scarcely yet got their eyes open, for they look frightened when they see a stranger! The women are masses of fat, and speak nothing but Cree; and dogs and Indians wander about the large, dark and filthy courtyard at pleasure.... Then no one can conceive the nuisance of the dogs. Each fort has a hundred or two of these devils, which ... are necessary for the winter sleighing, and these roam about searching for food (they are never fed), the courtyard being a perpetual scene of growling, snarling, and yelping all day, and of lamentable howling choruses all night. The plains, the plains for me.

The whole routine of a fort was "broken by the advent of a stranger at the board." And how much more so when that stranger was the governor himself, come to inspect their work. The best viands would be brought out — "the buffalo hump, tender and juicy; the moose nose, tremulous and opaque as a vegetable conserve; the finest and most savoury waterfowl; and the freshest fish — all preserved by the power of frost instead of salt." The governor had also brought his supplies, the goods rarely seen in a lonely post — "a lavish spread of delicacies from the Old World, bought by the governor himself," all luxuries in the frozen north.

And all were eager to hear the news from the outside world — what was happening in the fur trade, the newly formed Union, the new order about to be established by this unfamiliar governor, what was to be their fate.

As Simpson put it, "mirth is the order of the Day, but of course united with wisdom." Simpson would hold the attention with his endeavor to coil out a few tough yarns to the delight of the clerks and factor. Those who had never met him would have been surprised, if they hadn't already heard, that their governor was one of the most pleasant men they had ever seen.

In the evening the dance was held, with jigs and reels ruled over by the fiddlers. These were egalitarian affairs to which all were invited, including "all the dusky maidens within a hailing distance of the Fort," all met on terms of the most democratic equality.

From Cumberland House, Simpson travelled to Moose Lake, Swan River and the Upper Assiniboine, Fort Qu'Appelle, and Brandon House, during which arrangements were made to close the old NWC posts and keep the Bay posts. Simpson believed that even "trifling information is useful and can only be acquired by personal survey of the Country." So his visit was to acquaint himself with the trading stations in person, and to introduce the new system of economy and regularity to the traders.

Simpson's method of inspection assured that little was left to be learned by the end of a visit. How he did it was explained years after he had taken control, by the Sixth Earl of Selkirk, and demonstrates how Simpson was able to use his personality to gain knowledge in the fur posts:

> [Simpson] has such tact in seeing peoples characters that there is not a man in the country that he cannot lay down on paper at once, and tell what they are good for. In visiting a post he first has his talk with the chief in command, then with each of the under strappers down to the guides and interpreters, and never omits to go and have a gossip with the old women, so that before the canoe is gummed and in the water again, he is up to everything great and small that has happened at the post for a twelvemonth past, or since his last visit.

On his first inland trip, Rich says, Simpson "showed real statesmanship" by bringing Cuthbert Grant back into the service. Grant had been the Métis leader at the Massacre at Seven Oaks in 1816, and for that he had been shunned at the Union. Simpson described Grant as "a very stout, powerful fellow of great nerve and resolution ... [with] great influence over the half breeds and Indians." And that's why Simpson brought him back in.

Grant was of inestimable value to the Company, keeping the peace, preventing illicit trade with Americans, and providing meat for the settlers and pemmican for the Company canoe brigades. It was a generous and yet a shrewd choice of a doubtful man by the governor. Simpson was quite cynical about his purpose in promoting him: it "prevents him from interfering in the Trade on his own account ... it moreover affords us the benefit of his great influence over the half breeds and Indians of the neighborhood."

Simpson's appointment rehabilitated the reputation of this mercurial man. For many years Grant continued as the leader of the buffalo brigade. In 1834 he was made a justice of the peace and magistrate for Assiniboia, and in 1839 a councillor and sheriff. He rewarded Simpson's appointment by faithfully working to keep the Métis and Natives in check during the thirty years before his death in 1854. He is considered to be "the first Métis to wield a profound influence over the fate of his people." For that, much of the credit must go to Governor George Simpson.

In the winter of 1822–23, Simpson made his second trip, this time north to Lake Athabasca, up the Peace River, across to Lesser Slave Lake and the Athabasca River, then cut through the forests to Edmonton House (modern Edmonton). By such travelling, Simpson explained, "it frequently happens that a stranger perceives many things which from custom escape the observation of long residents."

By his inquiry into the most insignificant detail, Simpson gained an extraordinary knowledge of what was happening in his department. On his two circuitous winter trips of 1821–22 and 1822–23, Simpson had visited all of the major posts under his command east of the mountains.

This second trip was not just to oversee the Company's operations. Simpson was testing a new route he had in mind, one that he would work out in detail on his Columbia journey two years later.

In 1823 Simpson was faced with some alarming news. The Yankton Sioux were planning an attack on Red River Settlement from the United States. The attack had been provoked by a half-Sioux Métis named Joseph Rainville, who was demanding payment for some furs.

Although the threat of an attack "struck both the Indians and Settlers of Red River with consternation," Simpson "could not get a man to Volunteer." So he rounded up a rag-tag "army" — the missionary minister John West, the seventeen-year-old artist Peter Rindisbacher, and a few Company men. As Simpson explained: "I at length prevailed upon 30 hired Meurons who together with Gentlemen and servants amounted to about 50 in all [who] accompanied me well prepared for the worst." With this small contingent, Simpson set out from Red River for the international border at Pembina, fifty miles to the south.

Simpson's opposition was none other than the warrior chief Wanata, whose Sioux name means "The Animal Who Charges." He was "decidedly the greatest Indian chief of modern times — a tall man, being upwards of six feet high ... his features ... regular and well-shaped, his manners dignified and reserved, his attitudes graceful and easy, an intelligence that beams through his eyes."

The threat facing Simpson and his little band must have been a fearsome sight. The missionary minister, John West, was there and paints a vivid picture. Forty horsemen "were seen marching over the plains, with several colours flying, towards the Colony fort. [With] something like military precision, many of them were of remarkably fine stature and well proportioned, their countenances stamped with fierce and barbarous expression.... All armed with either long knives, tomahawks, guns, or bows, they soon encircled and formed a guard for the Chief of the party." Wanata was dressed in "a splendid cloak of buffalo skins ... decorated with fine tufts of owl feathers ... a splendid necklace formed of about sixty claws of the grizzly bear, his face painted with vermilion; on his hair he wore nine sticks neatly cut and smoothed, and painted with vermilion; these designated the number of gunshot wounds he had received."

And before them stood Simpson in his best London suit and top hat, guns and pistols incongruously strapped across his barrel chest, surrounded by his ragtag crew. We can imagine, as he usually did in his talk with the Natives, that Simpson minced no words and spelled out consequences. He could have drawn a line in the sand, and perhaps did — in this case the forty-ninth parallel, on which they were standing, which separates the United States from British North America. That is your side, he might have said, the American side; this side is our side, the British side, and we will kill you if you dare to attack us on our side.

This was talk that Wanata could understand, and he, like Rainville, backed down "with assurances of their most perfect amity toward the Company and Colony."

Rainville and Wanata salved their humiliation and regained their pride in their own way. Out on the plains a few days later, Rainville — now safely on the American side — "attacked some Freemen ... killing one, wounded four, and stole ten Horses." And shortly after meeting with Simpson, "Wanite the Chief ... shot and scalped an Assiniboin close to our gates in the dusk of the Evening and instantly with the whole band took to flight."

The "peppery little Hudson's Bay Company official," as one writer described him, was left holding the field.

Whatever Simpson said to Wanata that day must have had a profound effect, because Wanata later became a friend of the Bay Company. Chief Factor Robert Campbell met him in 1833, and Wanata and his warriors formed a protective guard for Campbell, who was delivering sheep to Red River. Later, Wanata visited Red River Settlement in the most friendly manner, when the Company protected him against other tribes that sought to harm him.

Wanata was a formidable foe, the most daring and the bravest that the plains nations could put up against Simpson, the incident bearing the possibility of an international disaster. The fact that it goes unnoticed in American history, and receives only a footnote in the history of Rupert's Land, is a tribute to Simpson's genius in turning a dangerous confrontation into little more than a laughing matter.

Behind Simpson's courage was a carefully worked out policy of disengagement. Any incident between the Sioux and the Rupert's Land Métis would draw the attention of the United States government and bring in federal troops. Any trading establishment on the American side would bring all the discord that would follow opposition.

Simpson took swift measures to remove the source of the trouble. The post in the United States was closed. The Métis were moved away from the border to settle deeper inside British territory. The Pembina trading post was torn down and its timbers taken to Red River for rebuilding. In this way, Rich says, "Americans were repulsed without the Company transgressing the frontier." So ended Simpson's first international incident.

If George Simpson stood head and shoulders above those around him, as biographer Arthur Morton claims, nothing illustrates that better than the introduction of simple law and order to Red River Settlement.

The Colony of Assiniboia was centred around the forks of the Assiniboine and Red rivers, now modern Winnipeg. With his appointment as Northern Governor, Simpson was forced to turn his attention to the safety and well-being of the colony. With the Union, the settlement had filled with the many officers and men who had become redundant. Simpson himself had little use for the community, considering the colony in a sorry state:

> Red River ... assumes more the appearance of a receptacle for free booters and infamous characters of all description than a well regulated Colony, there is no law and regularity every Man is his own Master.... I therefore think it indespensably necessary for its future wellfare that a Code of Laws should be made.

While in 1819 the population of the settlement was only a few dozen, the population in 1821 stood at about five hundred, made up of about two hundred Selkirk settlers, one hundred de Meurons, and one hundred Swiss colonists. The rest were French voyageurs, Métis, Natives, and Orkneymen.

Simpson had nothing but contempt for members of the Council of Assiniboia. In his opinion, one was "disaffected," another "drunken," another "froth," another "timid and weak as a child," another "discontented and designing," and two others were "a pair of thieves." As a council they had "no public spirit nor general view towards the welfare and good government of the place," using its sessions instead "for a glass of grog and ended with a great many more than another."

As governor of Assiniboia, the Committee in London had sent over a nephew of John Henry Pelly, Robert Parker Pelly. The best that could be said was that he was "a young man, apparently not without parts, but totally without experience." But at least Pelly was sensible enough to do one right thing — he asked George Simpson to step in and help him.

If Simpson had no use for the members of the Council of Assiniboia, they were, on paper at least, the governing body of the colony, and Simpson was determined to bring them to their sense of duty. He established the legitimacy of the council by reading into the record their commissions. The Resolutions of the General Court of the HBC of May 29, 1822, defined the powers of the governors and established law courts. He also read into the record a letter from Lord Bathurst, Colonial Minister, putting the imprimatur of the Imperial Government upon them. That part of the charter giving the Company power to administer oaths was quoted and the councillors took their oaths. The office of sheriff was created and a sheriff was sworn in; a militia was created. Fifty special constables were appointed and Chief Factor Donald McKenzie was placed at their head as High Constable. Bailiffs were appointed and oaths written to be taken by all holding office in the government's service.

By these simple acts, Simpson had established the legitimacy of the Council of Assiniboia. Then all of this was posted, first at the gates of Forts Garry and Douglas, and later on the doors of the churches. Simpson wanted the people to be very aware of the laws they would thereafter live under.

Other simple remedies were applied, partly to fend off foreign intervention, partly to satisfy the disaffections of the colonist. Goods were sold to the settlers at cost, and this, said Arthur Morton, "did more to allay discontent than all the constabulary sworn in." A simple currency under Simpson's signature was introduced, and this currency could be exchanged in England at no charge. Coins were brought in from England to handle small transactions. A herd of cattle arrived to satisfy the Scottish farmers. And the disaffected colonists — the Swiss and the de Meurons — were encouraged to leave for the United States. But perhaps the canniest move of all was Simpson's tactic to bring Cuthbert Grant back into favour, to assuage the demands of the Métis.

And those councillors that Simpson despised, turned out, once their duty was shown to them, to be worthy of their office. In the course of time the Council of Assiniboia became known for its sense of justice and fair play, its reputation for integrity and honesty lasting well into the twentieth century, long after it had ceased to be.

The reign of law came to Red River under the even hand of Governor Simpson. Biographer Arthur Morton would later say:

> To Simpson must go the credit of establishing firmly the institution of law and order, primitive though they were, and of creating a machine of government calculated to run with tolerable smoothness.... Simpson's winter in Red River (1823–24), left the stamp of a master mind upon the colony.

In 1826, William Williams was recalled by the London Committee and Simpson appointed governor of the Southern Department as well as of the Northern. From that point on, Simpson was effectively governor-in-chief of all the HBC territories in North America.

Soon, it was reported that Governor Simpson was "on his way down to Temiscamingue & has shown the same activity going about in Canada as he did in the interior." Another would write, "from what I have seen, [Governor] Simpson is as you say the real Gentleman and man of business. The Canada business is undergoing a thorough reform, greatly to the interest of the Company. No change here yet but it will come in due course."

Simpson took to his doubled duties with the ease with which he had overcome the problems of the Northern Department and the Columbia.

On June 1, 1825 the Council approved everything that Simpson had done in Rupert's Land and on the Columbia. And the Council asked that a letter to Simpson be appended to the public record of the 1825 Minutes, with the request that it be brought to the attention of the Committee:

> We the undersigned ... tender you our most grateful acknowledgements for the devoted attention and unremitting exertions you have so uniformly evinced throughout your whole management, more particularly, for the great retrenchment and amelioration introduced by your trip inland in 1822; the spirited and disinterested manner in which you undertook that of last year to the Columbia, in which District your Personal influence, masterly arrangements and decisive measures, have already been productive of the happiest effects and have opened a field on which to act with confidence and whence to look forward with expectation.

Simpson did not let the occasion go without responding in kind:

> Gentlemen: your approbation of my public conduct ... inspires a feeling of pleasure and

> satisfaction in my mind which I am at a loss
> for language to express. … [I] could have
> done little towards attaining the object in view,
> had I not been favored with your liberal and
> Friendly support and uniformly steady co-
> operation … and to *our joint* endeavors under
> the enlightened direction of the Honorable
> Company can alone be ascribed the present
> flattering appearance of our affairs.

And so on to the point of embarrassment. But the point was made. If the Council was divided, recalcitrant, opposed, or ever doubted the direction of George Simpson at the Union, it was now in lockstep with the goals of the HBC and the leadership of its new governor.

A year later the Governor and Committee in London added their own high praise:

> We consider the Fur Trade is very much
> indebted for its prosperous state to your tal-
> ents for distinct businesslike arrangement, and
> to your indefatigable zeal and perseverance.…
> We consider that you have acquired a more
> perfect knowledge of the Indian Trade than
> perhaps was ever possessed by any one indi-
> vidual or even by any body of Men who have
> been engaged in it.

In this atmosphere of glowing back-patting all round, George Simpson took the ship of the season back to London for a well-earned holiday, and so he could report in person to the

Committee. On Simpson's first years as governor, biographer Morton wrote:

> It was the first great achievement of George Simpson as Governor that he led the two factions into a common loyalty to one another, and to the Company. This he accomplished by the friendliness of his manner and disposition, by his even handed, impersonal administration, and by a strict discipline. That he stood head and shoulders in ability above those around him, that his office gave him almost supreme control in the country, and that he was the usual medium of communication with the Governor and Committee in London, the final authority in all matters, prevented the emergence of the old faction fight in the Council of the Northern Department.

5

Columbia:
"A Spirit of Enterprize"

Command ... only requires a spirit of enterprize
— George Simpson

When George Simpson completed his first overland journeys of 1821–22 and 1822–23, he wrote reports that were sent to the HBC in London. The Committee received these and duly noted their receipt. Then they vanished. They must have been exciting narratives, full of all the excitement and drama that George could devise. Perhaps someone took them home for his personal reading and forgot to return them — the story of borrowed books everywhere.

Fortunately for us, the record of his third great overland journey of 1824–25, from Fort York on Hudson Bay to Fort George on the Pacific and his return to Red River — a whirlwind journey of some 4,300 miles — has survived. We can follow him day by day, watching him deal with the myriad problems that still vexed the old Company, and enjoying himself along the way. The journal shows us Simpson in action, why he travelled, how he governed — a lesson in successful leadership.

He was an experienced traveller by this time, eager to set records, to travel faster than anyone ever had, or ever will. He had set up a race of sorts. He himself would explore the Burntwood-Beaver route. He gave John McLoughlin a twenty-day head start on the Hayes–Beaver route (McLoughlin bragged that Simpson wouldn't overtake him until west of the Rockies). And John Rowand had been sent at the same time as Simpson by the Hayes–Saskatchewan route. The end of the race would be Simpson's new Fort Assiniboine on the Athabasca River.

The whole prospect whetted his appetite for challenge, for it required thinking on a transcontinental scale, and brought him into opposition with the two greatest powers on Earth after England — the United States and the Russian Empire.

Courtesy of Library and Archives Canada. C-150743.

Hudson's Bay Company officials in express canoe, crossing lake. Artist Peter Rindisbacher (1806–1834).

* * *

York Factory, Sunday, August 15, 1824

Having waited in vain for the arrival of the ship of the season, and seeking to "ensure a passage to the Rocky Mountains before the Navigation closed," Simpson left York Fort bound for Fort George at the mouth of the Columbia. He was accompanied by "Chief Trader Macmillan in a North Canoe with a compliment of Eight Men besides my own Servant and an Indian Guide."

Simpson's purpose in Rupert's Land was to explore the Nelson River–Burntwood route — one not commonly used, and Simpson wanted to find out why. This meant rounding Marsh Point from York Factory into Hudson Bay, then entering the Nelson River, nearly two miles to the north. But Simpson's sanguine hopes for this route were almost immediately dashed:

> [I]n the very outset of the Voyage we had the misfortune to encounter a strong Gale of Wind…. We were obliged to put ashore, the tide running so high that in order to save the canoe it became necessary to get into the Water up to our Necks and there hold our weak bark until the Lading was taken up to the Beetch when she was carried ashore. [As a consequence the crew] shouldered our Craft and Baggage for Fifteen long Miles, [after which] we were still in sight of the Factory Smoke across the Point.

Split Lake, August 20

If George had thought it necessary to use the "broom and the prooning fork" on the Columbia, he would not have to wait until then. Almost immediately he found opportunities to clean house. At Split Lake, he found a clerk "so extremely inattentive that no duty can be entrusted to him; the very sight of an Indian he detests, he cannot live on the ordinary provisions of the country, he cannot even keep the common accounts or Memoranda of a Trading Post. He cannot command the people, he can neither venture on Snow Shoes nor in a small canoe, cannot provide a meal for himself with a Gun, and it would be certain Death to trust him out of doors in the severity of Winter."

This was no man for the fur trade. "I therefore," concluded Simpson, "in justice to the Young Man ... recommended his giving in his resignation as he is in no way adapted for the country, and a passage was immediately provided ... for the purpose of going home by the ship of this season."

Nelson House, August 24

By now Simpson was unrecognizable, a "*great man* in a long beard, Check Shirt which had once been green but which had assumed a different Colour in the muddy portage." Here Simpson discovered a boy of twelve or thirteen who had been on the payroll "these last *Six Years*," a form of abuse that had characterized the Company before the union, and now had to be stamped out. The route now turned into a maze of waterways for which no one knew the way. Fortunately, to Simpson's "inexpressible delight ... [he] discovered an Indian canoe as it was disappearing behind an island." Within an hour, Simpson had his guide, who led them to Frog Portage.

Frog Portage, August 30

Simpson was surprised to find that Chief Factor Clarke had left his brigade to enjoy some extra recreation at Norway House, and trade goods had been damaged by his careless crew. Next year at Council, Clarke was made to pay for the lost goods from his private account. At Lake Primeau he found that the Indians "were nearly starving being destitute of Ammunition. This says little for the management of affairs in English [River District]."

Now Simpson could report with considerable satisfaction: "I learnt that the Dr. [McLoughlin] had passed Ten Days ago so in that distance between York and this place we have gained Ten Days on him." The race was starting to heat up.

Île-à-la-Crosse, September 5

Simpson discovered that furs were trapped in the summer, and that the "unseasoned skins [were] not worth the prices paid for them." Moreover, he said, "the excuse of a Scarcity of ammunition is inadmissible as such scarcity is the clearest proof of extreme mismanagement and want of foresight." Simpson left Île-à-la-Crosse on September 6 at sunset, the weather "cold, raw, and disagreeable thick fogs and raining at intervals Daily." If that wasn't enough, Cadotte, the guide, tapped the liquor keg and got drunk. The road became nearly impassable. The Little Beaver River was "nearly dry … so that we were obliged to carry the Baggage along Shore while two men took the canoe up light with great difficulty." The Beaver River was worse, "many parts of it not even having the appearance of moisture," so that it was necessary to follow a difficult Indian track to Lac la Biche.

Lac la Biche, September 21

Here Simpson discovered that the Freemen "were preparing to go on a War Expedition against a poor helpless inoffensive tribe of Indians … with a view to plunder and gain themselves renown as Warriors by taking a few Scalps without incurring danger." Simpson had to read the riot act: "I … spoke my mind very plainly to these freemen, told them we meant to protect them [Indians] and if they did not instantly abandon their cruel intentions they should not this Winter have even a particle of ammunition … that next Summer they would be bundled down to Canada where starvation and misery would follow them." Thus the bloodshed was prevented, which, without Simpson's timely arrival, would have ended in a massacre. But Simpson did not leave it at that: "With Cardinal the freeman I made an agreement that in the course of this ensuing Winter and Spring get a horse Track or road cut from Fort Assiniboine to Edmonton House." The importance of this move will be seen on Simpson's return in 1825.

River la Biche, September 22
The river leading to the Athabasca River proved a "disagreeable navigation," having been "recently overrun by Fire and while still smoking a light rain had fallen so that we were up to the knee every step in Charcoal and ashes." However, amid the soot and smoke, he wrote, "we killed a fine fat buck Moose…. The Moose was soon relieved of his skin, a rousing fire made and all hands employed to the utmost [of] their skill in the art of Cookery; a haunch, the Nose, and Tongue Mr. Macmillan laid aside for ourselves and the rest of the animal made over to the people, who were occupied from the time of putting ashore … until the following morning in a continued succession of Eating, roasting, and boiling."

River la Biche, October 26
Simpson came upon the camp of Dr. John McLoughlin, the new chief factor of the Columbia District. Simpson waxed eloquent in describing this spectre:

He was such a figure as I would not like to meet on a dark Night in one of the by lanes in the neighbourhood of London, dressed in Clothes that had once been fashionable, but now covered with a thousand patches of different Colors, his beard would do honor to the chin of a Grizzly Bear, his face and hands evidently Shewing that he had not lost much time at the Toilette, loaded with Arms and his own herculean dimensions forming a tout ensemble that would convey a good idea of the high way men of former days.

Simpson had made up twenty days on the slower travelling McLoughlin, to the latter's "surprise and vexation." Now the two men travelled together.

Athabasca River, September 28

The brigade reached the Athabasca River on September 27, put up for the day to repair the canoes, "which had got much shattered in the shoal water of Rivière la Biche." On September 28, it passed the future town site of Athabasca, Alberta, and they reached the Slave River on the 29th. On October 1, Simpson wrote: "our Guide and Shorkie had a boxing match but after 4 or 5 good rounds it was a drawn battle in consequence of my interference, being afraid they might hurt each other." The group arrived the following morning at Fort Assiniboine.

Simpson found that John Rowand, sent to meet him there, had been, waited, and had gone, demonstrating "how much shorter the route is by the Saskatchawaine than by the Beaver River." Simpson informed the Committee that he had ordered this fort to be built and Cardinal, as we have seen, was ordered to cut a trail to Edmonton House. The troubles on the Nelson and Beaver rivers had already convinced Simpson that that route should be abandoned in favour of the Saskatchewan.

Simpson wrote that he left Fort Assiniboine at daybreak on October 3, and shortly after met "old Burleigh" coming downriver on a raft. Here was a man who caught Simpson's sympathetic eye. Once a great hunter, Burleigh had fallen on hard times. It seems he had "amassed a Fortune of about £7,000 and returned to Canada, but so enchanted was he with the roving Life of a Freeman and the charms of some half Doz[en] Wives ... that he could not sit down quietly at Home to enjoy his good Fortune but must revisit the Indian country, since which time he has met with nothing but reverses; his money disappeared, his talent as a hunter forsook him, and as he advanced in years, Wife after Wife deserted him, the last having given him the slip this morning, taking with her his favorite Child." Simpson could only feel compassion for this unfortunate man. He advised him to return to Canada "with the Wreck of his Fortune" and offered to "provide him with a passage free of expence."

Jasper's House, October 10–12
Simpson entered the mountains, on the trail of David Thompson, who had explored the route across the mountains in 1811. Here he met Jacco Findley, Thompson's helper thirteen years before. He was in Simpson's bad books: he had caught "Jacco Findlay and a band of followers (freemen) watching the Shewhoppes [Shuswaps, a Native tribe] in order that they might trade their Furs before they got to the establishment." These were middle-men in a monopoly country. Simpson gave them notice that "this nefarious Traffick" must be ended, and wrote letters to the nearby factors to "narrowly watch the conduct of Findlay's band."

The next day was occupied in preparations for attacking this formidable portage; that is, the Athabasca Pass, which would occupy the next week: "Sent Tho[ma]s McKay and six men ahead of us this morning in order to build a Canoe as the two craft laying there are not sufficient to take the whole of our party down the heavy rapids of the Columbia."

Athabasca Pass, October 14

"On the morning of the 14 we started in a body with a cavalcade of Twenty-one Horses," leaving the river to begin the climb over the mountains; the "scenery Wild and Majestic," the track nearly impossible. It crossed Simpson's wondering mind "how any human being [he is talking about David Thompson, of course] should have stumbled on a pass through such a formidable barrier." This was high praise for Thompson, a traveller who endured hardships no less toilsome than Simpson.

Summit, Athabasca Pass, October 17

At the summit at last, they discovered "a small circular lake ... which empties itself in opposite directions and may be said to be the source of the Columbia and Athabasca Rivers.... That this basin should send its waters to each side of the continent ... I thought it should be honored by a distinguishing title and it was forthwith named 'The Committee's Punchbowl.'" This was a joke for his London Committee, who, when reading Simpson's report, had a large punch bowl on its table dispensing liquor in all directions.

West Side of the Mountains, October 17–27

Now the party plunged down the west side of the mountains, "in many places nearly perpendicular," the land suddenly transformed from a stunted wilderness to "the most noble trees I ever beheld." After three days of struggle through the jungle of forest and river, Boat Encampment, at the great bend of the Columbia River, was reached.

Southward, the rate of descent, Simpson estimated, must be "100 miles per diem," plunging headlong through the Rapids of Death, past the future town of Revelstoke, through the Arrow Lakes, and into the lower Columbia, now in the United States. There the group found chief trader Ogden, who "represents the Country to be in a state of Peace and quietness and the Company business going on as usual." To which Simpson scoffed:

> [That] is not saying a great deal as if my information is correct, the Columbia Department from the Day of its origin to the present hour has been neglected, shamefully mismanaged and a scene of the most wasteful extravagance and the most unfortunate dissention. It is high time the system should be changed and I think there is ample field for reform and amendment.

Spokane House, October 28

Simpson detoured sixty miles on horseback to Spokane House, from whence the Snake Country Expedition set out. Simpson found that the hunt was conducted in the summer, not in the winter when the "fur-bearing animals are in their prime." A "worthless and motley crew" was left idle for the winter, their outfits used up and their horses consumed for food before the hunt began. These freemen, Simpson concluded, were "a most unruly and troublesome gang to deal with," and Mr. Alexander Ross, the expedition leader, "has not the talent and ... his

presence among them has been attended with little good....
The important duty should not in my opinion be left to a self-
sufficient empty-headed man like Ross ... whose reports are so
full of bombast and marvellous nonsense that it is impossible
to get any information that can be depended upon from him."

Ross may not have been a great fur trader, in Simpson's
opinion, but Simpson did not send him packing. Instead, Ross
was removed from the fur trade but offered a position at Red
River Settlement. Ross was to become one of the most respected
citizens of Red River, the historian of the western fur trade
before Simpson, the historian of Red River Settlement, a councillor and magistrate of the colony.

With Ross removed, Simpson suggested that Chief Trader
Peter Skene Ogden undertake the Snake River campaign, and
he did so with "utmost readiness." Ogden's instructions were
simple: "the country is a rich preserve of Beaver and which for
political reasons we should endeavour to destroy as soon as possible." This was a major tactical move, as Simpson planned to set
up a buffer wasteland between the HBC and the Americans.

From Spokane House, Simpson returned to the Columbia,
and on October 8, 1824, arrived at Fort George, "having performed the Voyage from Hudson's Bay across the continent of
America to the Northern Pacific Ocean in 84 days thereby gaining
twenty days on any Craft that ever preceded us."

Fort George, Mouth of the Columbia, October 9, 1824, to March 15, 1824

Simpson now summed up the problems facing him:

> I cannot help thinking that no œconomy has
> been observed, that little exertion has been

used, and that sound judgment has not been
exercised but that mismanagement and extravagance has been the order of the day. It is
now, however, necessary that a radical change
should take place and we have no time to lose
in bringing it about.

Now Simpson began the real work for which he had come
to the Columbia — a complete overhaul of the business on the
west coast. The extravagance of importing expensive European
goods for the officer was stopped. Locally grown foods would
take their place. Fort George was closed and a new fort
established upriver called Fort Vancouver, on the north side
of the river. Further up the river, Simpson established Fort
Colvile, which in time became the marshalling point for New
Caledonia and a food-producing establishment. Puget Sound
to the north was explored and Company farms begun there.
New Caledonia needed an outlet to the Pacific Ocean, so an
exploring party under the command of Chief Trader James
Macmillan was sent north to explore the lower Fraser River.
Exploring parties were sent south as far as California and
east as far as modern Utah and Idaho, where the rivers were
trapped clean of beaver.

Most importantly, Simpson had appointed a new chief
factor, John McLoughlin, an irascible, difficult man, but in
Simpson's judgment the man to bring order to the vast Columbia
Department.

Native tribes on the west coast were large and warlike, and
had not yet learned to live in peace with whites. Tribes soon
learned that men who killed a white man would be hunted down
and killed, that trading posts would be moved away from their

convenience. When travelling through coastal waters, heavily armed brigades made attack impossible.

A new Fort Langley on the Fraser would receive returns from New Caledonia and supply the Coasting trade with goods. This plan depended on the Fraser River being navigable to its upper reaches, and for that purpose Simpson would return in 1828 to explore the river.

At sea, Simpson would "put down all opposition of the Coast" and take over the provisioning of the Russian posts in the north. Idle hands would be sent exploring north and south to "acquire a knowledge of the Coast natives and Country."

Simpson informed the Committee that McMillan's expedition was "one of the principal objects I had in view in visiting the Columbia," in order to "make one department of the whole west side of the Mountain."

Fort Vancouver, Saturday March 19, 1825

Simpson then began his return trip. By the nineteenth the brigade had arrived at that point in the river where Simpson had ordered a new headquarters to be built. It was well along to completion:

> [A]t sun rise mustered all the people to hoist the flag staff. In presence of the gentlemen ... I baptized it by breaking a bottle of rum on the flag staff and repeating the following words in a loud voice: "In behalf of the Honourable Hudson's Bay Company I hereby name this establishment Fort Vancouver. God save King George the 4," with three cheers.

Walla Walla, March 27

At Walla Walla a crisis had developed. The interpreter had been overly intimate with the Native women and his "indiscreet amours ... incited the natives against us.

"It is a lamentable fact," Simpson complains, "that almost every difficulty we have with the Indians throughout the country may be traced to our interference with their Women ... 9 murders out of 10 committed on whites by them have arisen through Women." To end this particular crisis, Simpson took the interpreter across the mountains for a few years to keep him out of harm's way.

Simpson's fame had now spread. Nine chiefs had gathered at Walla Walla to hold a conference with him:

> I made them a speech occupying about two hours, gave them a dram and fathom of tobacco, 50 ball and powder each, and about 33 fathoms tobacco for the general use of the camp.... Four hours and many pipes of tobacco were consumed in the Council.... We parted excellent friends.

At Kettle Falls, where Simpson wished to establish his new trading post, he was careful to have the full agreement of the chief. "I went to the Chiefs Lodge," Simpson related, and "had an interview with him and some of his principal followers and intimated to him my wish to form an Establishment on his Lands provided he undertook to protect it and assured us of his Friendly disposition." The chief "received the proposal with much satisfaction and offered me the Choice of his Lands.... We selected a beautiful point on the South side.... An excellent farm can be made at this place." Simpson himself paced off the establishment of 150 feet square, and named it Fort Colvile. Then he made a speech of about an hour's length, "as they estimate harangues by measurement." Fort Colvile would become, in the course of time, a major food supplier on the upper Columbia.

The journey continued. But after a winter on the mild Pacific coast, his men were not in the best of shape. Five laboured under "Chinook Love Fever," while another seven had been sent back for the same reason. His crew ill, Simpson himself became the food provider, killing a red deer to supply meat for the men, and a welcome treat: "four hours ashore is still the order of the night and our voracious Canadians seem disposed to make one 'pipe' of it in the eating way until the signal is given for being under weigh."

Boat Encampment, April 22

Now began the most arduous portage Simpson would ever suffer in his long career — the notorious Athabasca Pass in deep snow, forty-five miles in a straight line, but seventy-five by the twisting trail. If there were no horses, Simpson commented, "we shall have to make use of our Legs." If there was no food, the men would go hungry until they got to the other side. And so began the laborious climb up the face of the Rocky Mountains. "The Governor himself, generally at the head, made the first plunge into the water, and was not the last to get out. His smile encouraged the others, and his example checked murmuring," said Ross, who was with the brigade. Problems developed almost at once. Some slackers had lagged behind and "broached the keg of rum [of] which all partook except some of my own crew and about half a dozen of them were so drunk that they could not come on." So Simpson left them behind (they were sent back for the next day). One Native threw away his baggage, and Simpson gave him a beating with a stick on the spot. "And further to mark my displeasure of the conduct of our people this day, I knocked a Hatchet into the head of our rum Keg and dashed the contents into the river." By now the men were lame from wading across the ice-cold river, and exhausted by the climb, but Simpson drove them on.

Committee's Punch Bowl, Summit, April 25

At last they made it to the top, to the Committee's Punch Bowl that had greeted them so pleasantly the year before. At this point "every man [was] lame & exhausted," and to mark their arrival, Nature sent an enormous avalanche careening down the side of the mountain above them. Now, on the shores of the Punch Bowl, Simpson gave each man a little rum, "which was drunk to the health of our Honours and three cheers," a tribute, Alexander Ross recalled, "always paid to this place when a nabob of the trade passes by."

On April 26 Simpson began the descent to the eastern side, and "never did exhausted travellers turn out less disposed to re-new a toilsome Journey ... every man of the party requiring a walking stick, our feet being much blistered and Lacerated." Repeated fords of the icy river led them downward. Then, a joyful shout as horses were sighted, and the men put up for breakfast. But the news from the east is of disaster: Norway House had burnt down and the Red River settlers had no grain for their crops. Instead of resting his men, Simpson had to drive them on.

Fort Assiniboine, April 30

At his new fort, Simpson received some good news. The freemen he had hired at Lac la Biche the previous summer had done their job. The "new road" had been cut through the forests to Fort Edmonton, "tolerably good considering that it has been opened since I passed here last Fall through thick Woods."

Simpson's planning is paying off: "I am now from experience able to say that New Caledonia and Lesser Slave Lake can be supplied by this route instead of Athabasca and Beaver River." Simpson even did a little pleasant gloating: "I am satisfied that this discovery of Mine (as I alone can claim the merit thereof never having been even dreamt of by any other) will enable [the Company] to do the Peace River business at a reduction of one-third of the usual expences."

Fort Edmonton, May 2

At Edmonton, after a two-day rest, Simpson "gave the people a danse in the Evening," at which "all the people about the establishment, high and low, old and young of every class, attended, dressed in their best attire."

If the crossing of the mountains had been difficult, Simpson was now faced with another precarious situation. Although he wished to rest himself and his crew, events to the east made it necessary for him to travel on: "I have therefore determined on being off immediately." He knew the risks. In plains territory, it was not safe to travel with one boat, but, as he needed to get quickly to Red River Settlement, it was necessary in this case. Simpson concluded: "I therefore formed a plan the boldness of which induced the people to believe my senses had taken leave of me … no other than that of starting Forth … across Land to Red River Settlement, a distance according to our route computed at 800 miles by plains infested by the Most Warlike and hostile Tribes in North America."

The Prairies, May 5–28

Simpson left Edmonton House with a party of ten. It was necessary to travel light, so "for provisions we had to depend on our guns." Simpson almost gloried in the peril: "Never did a party undertake a dangerous Voyage so ill-prepared and never was there such a Voyage thereof undertaken in the Indian Country." At the warning of a local war party, Simpson argued, "it does not do for a Governor to appear shy." So the brigade camped early and "myself [Simpson] and two of the people took the first watch." Two days later, he wrote, "our guide today got quite bewildered and lost much ground by not keeping in the proper direction." Finally, the guide "[found] himself perfectly at home on the route," and the journey resumed. The routine was simple: "leave at four, travel five hours, breakfast and give the horse two hours rest then travel three hours, lay by until 4 o'clock and then go on until dusk.... Our walk is a steady 3½ to 4 miles per hour, horses only to carry goods and provide food if necessary."

On May 15, Simpson's servant, Tom Taylor, and a friend left the party on a hunting expedition. When they did not return, Simpson declared them lost and left them behind: "I am obliged to give them up as lost to us for this Voyage." (The two men found their own way out and were reunited with Simpson at Norway House.)

By May 21 the party was in great difficulty: "Ourselves and horses were really in a state of great distress throughout the day by the unceasing persecution of the Muschetoes bleeding us at every accessible pore." As if that weren't enough, the party encountered violent thunderstorms and were "drenched [with] torrents of rain."

At the forks of the Assiniboine and Qu'appelle rivers the waters were so high that fording was impossible. A fearless Simpson came to the rescue:

The Water was too deep to Wade, there was no wood of any kind to make a raft, several of our people could not swim, and the bottom and banks [were] so soft that there was the utmost danger of drowning or miring our horses; in the dilemma we had nearly resolved on killing our horses & making skin canoes of the Hides for the purpose of going down to the settlement by water. I, however, being more at home in the water than any of my fellow travellers and anxious to save the lives of the poor animals, stripped and swam across with a few things. Others followed my example and by making several crossings in this way we got the whole of our little baggage over; the horses were driven over, those people who could not swim holding on to their tails and with the assistance of cords we hauled the poor animals out of the water.

Safely across, the governor indulged in poetic melodrama: "In short I believe there never was an unfortunate Gov'r in such a Woeful plight as that of the Northern Department of Rupert's Land this Day."

Now lost among "Sandy Knowls," now passing "through a swamp nine miles in length, frequently up to the Waist in Mud and Water," the party reached White Horse Plains, fifteen miles west of Red River Settlement.

White Horse Plains, Saturday May 28

Though only a half day's march from Red River, the men were too exhausted to continue. Simpson sent to Fort Garry for horses, from whence "they instanter dispatched Men, Horses, Eatables, Drinkables, and dry cloaths." But George was to end his epic journey in a "Grand Stand finish," as Rich puts it.

Simpson writes that, while the men rested, he "got across my old charger 'Jonathan,' gave him the Rein with a smart cut across the haunches, and commenced a furious attack upon the gates of Fort Garry at 12 P.M. ... after having performed one of the most dangerous and harassing Journeys ever undertaken in the Country through which, thank God, I have got with no injury or inconvenience worthy of Notice."

Of this final flourish, historian Rich comments:

> The last gallop to Fort Garry was evidence of the natural leadership and power of the man. It was just the kind of bravado which appealed to those whom he had to lead and to dominate. Who, even the hardest-bitten fur traders, would dare to challenge a man who could make such a journey, and finish it in such style?

This is a great adventure story. Where else in literature can we find a true story of a man coursing a continent and transforming it along the way? And having the time of his life while doing it? Certainly when Simpson planned his trip he had a pretty good idea of what he hoped to accomplish: to transform the West. In time he reorganized the transportation routes both in Rupert's Land and on the Pacific slope. He drove out the Americans in the Snake River country as well as from the coastal trade (in order to take over the provisioning of the Russian posts further north). He moved the headquarters to a reliable deep-water port and imported shipping for both the coastal and deep-sea trade.

Behind all this manoeuvring was his intent to join the Columbia and New Caledonia into one vast department.

Simpson brought his ideas to fruition by a tangible and clearly defined course of action. Once on the coast, Simpson's mind worked to deal with all the problems he faced, and as usual he went at them methodically, one by one: the lack of enterprise in exploration; the weak response to the Americans both on land and sea; the realities of the division of the territory yet to come; the pacification of the Native tribes; the effective use of what Simpson called "the broom and the prooning fork" to weed out the lazy, the worn out, the ineffective, and the trouble-makers. In all of this we see the masterly handling of men, whether his traders, the chiefs, or his voyageurs, even the troublemakers he brought back with him. And from the other side, of course, is the loyalty and confidence these men had in Simpson's leadership.

He had performed remarkable feats, not only of physical stamina but in managerial genius. Whether as adventurer or reformer, it was a performance never to be equaled or repeated in North America. Simpson had taken huge steps to secure the safety of British North America on the West Coast, which, followed up successfully by Simpson himself, and later Sir James Douglas, secured New Caledonia, now British Columbia, for Canada.

This is an adventure story that should make Simpson as famous as Lewis and Clark are in the United States. But in Canada his voyage is barely mentioned as a footnote in fur-trade history. The expeditions of both Mackenzie and Lewis and Clark had to overcome great geographical challenges to accomplish their ends. But except in symbolic terms, to be worked out later by history, neither transformed the political landscape at the same time. Simpson did that, but his accomplishment has never received the public acclaim it merits.

* * *

Simpson's plan for the reorganization of the West Coast depended on the Fraser River being navigable for canoes. In 1828 Simpson returned to the West to explore the possibilities of the river. He shot both the Thompson River and Fraser Canyon, "like the flight of an arrow," only to come to a disheartening conclusion: "Frazers River can no longer be thought of as a practicable communication with the interior."

This was a blow that Simpson had not expected, a great blow to his plans for a smoothly running trade from New Caledonia to the ships on the coast. Trade continued to pass through Fort Vancouver until 1846, when the border was fixed at the forty-ninth parallel. Then a difficult road was cut from the Okanogan to the Fraser, along much the same route as the present Hope–Princeton Highway.

But Simpson was right in the long run. Of the two great rivers flowing to the Pacific, it would be the Fraser, not the Columbia, that would become the great carrier of commerce. After the fur trade, the upper Columbia fell into disuse, while in the course of time two railway lines and a highway were driven through the Fraser Canyon. Simpson's thinking was sixty years ahead of his time.

Simpson arrived back at Lachine on August 27, 1829. He then sailed from New York on September 24 and was in London to be introduced to the Governor and Committee on October 21.

Simpson was by this time a formidable governor. He administered an empire extending from Labrador to the Pacific. He had quartered his territories on four great journeys and had imposed an order which no one disputed. By then the councils of the Northern and Southern Departments were agreeable, the posts were run with an economy and efficiency as never before, and the Committee in London routinely endorsed his policies.

There was little need to travel at the pace of former days. The frontiers had been explored, the rapids and the cascades run. Now he could enjoy some of the fruits of his labours. At thirty-six years of age, George Simpson had thoughts of a church wedding.

The next five years would be unhappiest of his life.

6

Marriage: Many Tender Ties

*The many tender ties, which find a
way to the heart.*
— *James Douglas*

Once established as governor, Simpson quickly brought an end
to the system of multiple liaisons and concubinage that had prevailed in the past. Resolutions of Council laid down new stan-
dards for family relations in Rupert's Land. Effectual civilization and moral improvement of officers' families would ensure
that women and children received religious instruction; that
children would be taught their ABCs; that "irregularity, vicious
or indolent habits" would be "checked and discountenanced";
that "the mother & children always be addressed and habitu-
ated to converse in the vernacular dialect (whether English or
French) of the Father." And in a celebrated resolution "none

be hereafter allowed to take a women without binding himself down to such reasonable provision and maintenance of her as on a fair and equitable principle may be considered necessary."

Women sometimes abandoned their husbands to go with another man, but officers of the Company wishing to end a relationship had to support the woman and any children until she remarried. (George's wife, Margaret Taylor, received £30 a year until her marriage to Amable Hogue.)

George Simpson married early in his life, changing partners five times.

In London when he was twenty-two years of age, George fathered a daughter, Maria Louisa, born in October 1815. Another child named Isabella was born, probably in 1819. The name of the mother of Maria Louisa is known to be Maria, and this woman may have been the mother of Isabella, as well, but we can't be sure of that. Just what arrangement Simpson made for her and the children is unclear now, but it seems (assuming that Isabella is from the same mother) to have been stable and relatively long-lasting. The relationship was no secret, and Simpson could joke about it with his friends. Whatever provisions were made, they would have been seen as accepted and proper conduct for a young bachelor in the mercantile world.

Shortly after he arrived in Rupert's Land, Simpson married Elizabeth Sinclair, daughter of Chief Factor William Sinclair, an Orkneyman, her mother unknown. She must have been a personally attractive young woman; however, the relationship does not appear to have worked out, and a marriage was arranged for her with the "ridiculously stiff and stately" Robert Miles, Simpson's clerk in the Athabasca. Elizabeth lived out the rest of her life with Miles, first at York Factory, then on East Main, then in retirement in Ontario. She died March 3, 1878, and is buried near Brockville, Ontario.

Her marriage to George resulted in one child, Maria Simpson, who was raised by Simpson at Red River Settlement. The story of Maria is one of the most tragic in Rupert's Land. At the age of sixteen she married a young English botanist, Robert Wallace, and the two joined a canoe brigade travelling to the Columbia. While running dangerous rapids on that river, young Wallace panicked, grabbed his wife and jumped into the water to save her. In doing so he tipped the canoe; he and his wife perished, along with ten others, including at least four children.

In 1824 Simpson married Jane Klyne, the daughter of French-Canadians Michel Klyne and Suzanne Lafrance. She accompanied Simpson to Fort Vancouver and a child, James Keith Simpson, was born to her there. She then married Archibald McDonald, had many children by him, and died in St. Andrews, Quebec, in 1879.

When George Simpson returned to Rupert's Land from his sojourn in England in the spring of 1826, he married Margaret Taylor, the daughter of sloop master George Taylor of Berwick-upon-Tweed, England. They were married for four years, and George seems to have had a particular fondness for her. One of her sons described her as a "sturdy Scotswoman." In 1830, John Stewart, under whose care Margaret was then living, described her as "both decent and modest beyond anything I could expect, or ever witnessed in any of her country women ... she appears to be as contented as it is possible for one of her sex to be in the absence of their Lord and natural protector and as a mother she is most kind and attentive to her children. She is the quietest and best natured creature I ever met with."

She must have been a rare beauty, as well, as Simpson seems to have been enamoured of her as he was of no other woman in his life. Their first child, George Stewart Simpson, was born in 1827.

When George removed to Lachine for the winter of 1827–28 he may have taken Margaret with him; presumably it was Margaret living with Simpson that winter. If so, in 1828 she would have travelled back with him to Rupert's Land, and travelled on with him when he left for New Caledonia and the Columbia in August. The need for her companionship was great, and he could report the she "has been a great consolation to me."

At Fort Vancouver, about the end of November, she became pregnant with her second child. She travelled back to Rupert's Land with George in the spring, traversed the difficult Athabasca Pass on snowshoes, and continued on to Fort Edmonton. There George considered that Margaret, because of her advanced pregnancy, would be unable to keep up with the hectic pace he would be setting back to Red River. Margaret was left behind under the care of Chief Factor Rowand, later to be taken at a slower pace to Fort Alexander on the Winnipeg River, where she came under the care of Chief Factor John Stuart. Her second child, a boy, was born there on August 29, 1829, later baptized as John Mackenzie Simpson.

George's return to England at the end of 1829 had as one of its purposes the search for an English wife. But the search for an amiable companion in the civilized world was not to bring him the true comfort and happiness of the domestic life that he sought.

Margaret married Amable Hogue at Red River Settlement on March 31, 1831. Amable had been an oarsman on Simpson's express canoe, so Margaret had known him for several years before the marriage. She remained with Amable until his death in 1856, and stayed a widow for the next twenty-nine years. Margaret died in 1885 at the age of seventy-five, and is commemorated by a simple obelisk, which reads: MARGUERITE TAYLOR, WIFE OF AMABLE HOGUE, DIED DECEMBER 16, 1885.

Margaret has a special place in Canadian history that goes unmentioned. George boasted that during the summer of 1828 he had travelled seven thousand miles and was the first to complete a transcontinental voyage in one season, a record which still stands. But if Margaret was with him at Lachine during the winter of 1827–28, which is likely, then she completed the same transcontinental voyage, and would be the only woman ever to have completed the same passage in one season — perhaps ever. She certainly travelled with her husband from York Factory to the Columbia in 1828, and that, too, must stand as a record for a woman. But more impressive, she is probably the only woman ever to shoot the Fraser Canyon by canoe, and for this courageous deed she gets no credit at all.

The marriage of George Simpson to his cousin Frances Ramsay Simpson in 1830 was brokered by Frances's father, Geddes Mackenzie Simpson. A marriage contract was agreed to, marriage licence allegations were sworn to on February 18, 1830, and the marriage contract signed and sealed. The marriage ceremony of George Simpson and Frances Ramsay Simpson was held in St. Leonard's Church, Bromley on Stratford, on February 24, 1830.

In view of what was to follow, the wisdom of Geddes brokering his daughter's marriage to George, and of Frances's acceptance of the offer can be questioned. Both knew George as a boisterous socializer and traveller, and the workaholic governor-in-chief of a vast fur empire. Frances, on the other hand, was described as gentle and devoted to her family. It was hardly a combination likely to lead to the comfort of a domestic life that either sought, yet both seem to have loved each other well enough.

Image PDP02186 courtesy of Royal BC Museum, BC Archives.

Portrait of Sir George Simpson, Governor of the Hudson's Bay Company, by George Pearce. Simpson is shown standing in his Lachine office.

Frances's beauty shines out of a portrait taken when she was eighteen, but it fails to give any indication of her overall size. It's unlikely she was much more than five feet tall. George Simpson at five foot seven or more would have been much taller.

A few weeks after the wedding, George and Frances set sail for North America. Almost immediately upon departing from Liverpool, Frances was beset with seasickness so severe that George tried to bribe the captain to put them ashore in Ireland. It was an omen of things to come. "Seasickness, as many can attest," wrote biographer John Galbraith, "can be experienced by people in robust health, but the frailty she evidenced on the voyage was to be her most prominent characteristic throughout her married life." Frances recovered sufficiently to complete the voyage, landing at Boston on April 16, 1830. From there the couple travelled to Lachine and then left by the familiar canoe route for Rupert's Land. Since leaving England, Frances had kept a diary of her travels, and this was continued all the way across North America to York Factory.

What comes through in her diary is a picture of a young woman who, writes canoe enthusiast Grace Lee Nute, "not only kept her good humour, but actually seems to head the long list of those who find the voyageur's life a rewarding one." Though the ocean voyage incapacitated her, the canoe voyage filled Frances with an elation that shines through the pages of her diary. Everything seemed to interest and delight her — the little Native girl who presented her with "a Bouquet of Cherry Blossom very prettily arranged"; the voyageurs who "paddled, sung, laughed & joked as if on an excursion of pleasure"; the court martial of a would-be deserter sentenced to a dozen lashes, which would have been carried into effect had not "Mrs. McTavish and myself called to their aid our most persuasive arguments, and obtained their pardon"; the tumble that her fellow traveller Catherine McTavish experienced when, being carried through a swamp, her porter, Nicholas, in a scene "so ridiculous that the bystanders could not resist a laugh, in which Mrs. McTavish joined so heartily, that poor Nicholas ... stumbled forward, fell on his face and gave his unfortunate rider a summerset over his head, into the mud: throwing her into a situation, the most awkward that ever poor Lady was placed in."

This was a young woman thoroughly enjoying herself, by no means daunted by the stress of a continental canoe voyage, a voyage that before the summer was over, would take her three thousand miles from Lachine to Red River, then to York Factory and back to Red River.

After Frances's exhilaration of the canoe journey through the heart of the continent, a sedentary life at Red River was an anticlimax. However, Simpson set out to make his winter at Red River a memorable one for her. "We are all gaping for the arrival of some half-dozen great wigs," wrote Alexander Ross, "who are expected to pass their holy days with his excellency, which together with the fascinating accomplishments of Mrs. Simpson will give the place an air of high life & gaiety. We have already no few attractions, the painted house of state, the Pianoforte, & the new fashioned Government Carriole are objects to attract and amuse."

Winter was the time of play in Red River, when the carrioles came out painted in their garish colours, the dogs festooned with ribbons and a string of merry bells, all dashing through the settlement, along the river, and out onto the plains. "Mrs. Simpson enjoys a Red River winter and I myself am much better, thank God, than at any time for the last 12 months," Simpson wrote just before Christmas 1830. With the great wigs there, the dances and the feasts, Fort Garry and government house must have been filled with laughter and pleasure for Christmas and the New Year of 1831, as George arranged for "two or three grand let outs."

But the seeds of family disaster and despair had already been planted in early December of 1830, when Frances became pregnant. As it turned out she could not carry her pregnancies easily. She took to her bed with a malaise that the doctor could not understand. In the new year the results began to show on Frances's health. In early 1831 George wrote to his friend McTavish at Moose Factory: "You'll be sorry to learn that my poor wife is by no means in good health." The matter did not improve with the coming of spring. On April 10, 1831, Simpson wrote that Frances was "still seriously indisposed," and a month later that she "still continues a great invalid, the greater part of her time in Bed and the symptoms by no means favorable." As late as June 3, 1831, Simpson could write:

> My dear wife you will be sorry to learn is very unwell indeed, almost entirely confined to her bedroom and altho not in an immediately dangerous state much worse than Women generally are in such conditions, under such conditions it really breaks my heart to part from her.... She has been closely confined to bed for several days past.

The birth of the child, a boy named George Geddes Simpson, on September 2, 1831, brought joy to Frances and George, but the child was weak and his health had to be guarded with constant medical attention. And still the health of Frances did not improve. George wrote to McTavish on January 3, 1832:

> My poor wife had the most narrow escape imaginable; during the whole 9 months of her confinement she was in extreme ill health and so much reduced & weakened that at the crisis she was more Dead than alive; her recovery was exceedingly slow and she is still very thin and by no means strong. Our little boy was for a time ailing and delicate, but he is now picking up and promises well.

The successful birth of the child brought relief to the couple, and Simpson continued in his duties with the annual meeting of the Northern Council. But the closing in of another winter brought a recurrence of the symptoms that had caused so much concern a year before. On December 15, 1831, John Stuart wrote to James Hargrave to express his concerns:

> Unfortunately Mrs. Simpson is not well ... she has been ailing since Christmas and though her disease is not by the doctor considered dangerous I strongly apprehend that the climate of this country will not agree with her and that her stay cannot be much prolonged — this of course, if it happens, will also draw the Governor away and I know not a greater misfortune that could befall Red River.

The young heir continued in ill health, and on April 22, 1832 — Easter Sunday — the boy died. George related the details, his heart filled with agony:

> At her [Frances's] particular request I remained at home to have an eye over him as it was death to her when we were both absent, but she had scarcely got seated on her saddle when he was seized with violent retching on my knee, soon after became convulsed and breathed his last as she was in the act of crossing the threshold after pouring out her prayers for him at the Lord's Table.

The death was compounded by the remorse that struck Lady Simpson, feeling that she herself had caused the death. Years later she poured out her grief to Letitia Hargrave. "Poor Mrs. Simpson blamed herself," Letitia wrote, "for having dressed her baby in white in the English way, frocks made out of Nansook [light cotton].... It died of inflammation of the lungs."

The boy, for whom Simpson had such great hopes, was buried in St. John's Anglican Church in Red River. Years later, apparently after Simpson's death, someone raised a small stone to him, which reads: TO THE MEMORY OF GEORGE GEDDES SIMPSON, SON OF THE LATE SIR GEORGE SIMPSON, GOVERNOR OF THE HUDSON'S BAY COMPANY, DIED APRIL 22, 1832, AGED 8 MONTHS.

Rupert's Land was no place for an ailing governor, and it was no place for the sick Frances, who in March of 1833 had become pregnant again. With the death of George junior, Simpson's dream of a capital in the wilderness died. It was the lowest point in his life. His own illness was at a critical stage, his wife was pregnant, and he could not take the chances of medical attention available in Red River for the health of either of them. In retrospect, the sojourn at Red River had been a devastating mistake.

In the late spring of 1833, George took his ailing wife back along the old fur trade route, the same one that had given Frances so much pleasure only three years before. They passed Fort Coulonge on the Ottawa River on July 13, when John Siveright wrote that "our worth[y] Governor & Lady had improved in health when they passed here." Later, James McMillan reported that he was "glad to say that our worthy Gov. and Lady arrived safe at Lachine — and were to start for England on the 25 July. Mrs. Simpson was still in the same delicate state."

Donald Ross was pleased to write: "News has arrived of the Governor's safe arrival and departure from Montreal — he had himself improved much in health, but Mrs. Simpson was still very low."

And so they returned to London, his wife safe again at her parents' home at New Grove House on Mile End Road. But one voice stood out, that of Chief Factor J.D. Cameron, echoing the thoughts of Letitia Hargrave, the dread feeling of many, that the ordeal at Red River would have lasting consequences for Frances:

> He mentions his health as being much improved but still unable to attend to business — As for Mrs. Simpson, she was nothing better than when she left Red River. In fact, that Amiable Lady woman was too much Doctored in this country — and I am much afraid she will feel the effects of it as long as she lives.

Shortly after returning home, Frances gave birth to her second child, a girl named Frances Webster Simpson, on December 30, 1833.

When Simpson took his pregnant wife home from Rupert's Land in 1833, his life had plunged to the lowest period of his life. The boy child on whom he had placed so much hope was dead, his wife was devastated physically and emotionally, and George, too, was broken in spirit and in body. It was generally thought that he would retire from the trade.

The health of George and Frances improved slowly during the winter. In the spring of 1834, John Siveright wrote, "I am happy to hear [they both] had recovered their wonted good health, soon after their arrival in England. He was expected in Canada early in this month [April 1834] & I hope to see him pass in a few days on his way to the interior." Simpson returned to his duties in Rupert's Land, and resumed his domestic life from time to time on his visits home to England.

Though the winter in England had helped Simpson recover some of his health, he left still bearing the effects of his long illness. But when he returned in the fall of 1835, HBC secretary William Smith could only exclaim:

> Our friends the Governor with Chief Factor J. Keith made their appearance this morning via Liverpool by the Packet of the 1 [of October 1835].... The former has grown blooming again and looks ten years younger than when he left England, Spring 1834.

George Simpson was back in business.

* * *

Part of the motive in Simpson's marriage to Frances Ramsay Simpson was to elevate the moral tone of Rupert's Land by encouraging, by example, the marriage of his officers to English and Scottish women. By 1840, James Douglas, in the far-off Columbia District, could write, "there is a strange revolution, in the manners of the country; Indian women were at one time the vogue, the half breed supplanted those, and now we have the lovely tender exotic torn from the parent bed."

At a devastating cost to his own marriage and family plans, Simpson was successful. Almost immediately his officers began to look to the United Kingdom for wives. Governesses sent to teach at the Girls' Academy at Red River Settlement were quickly swept up by Company officers. Far to the west, Jane, the wife of Chief Factor Archibald McDonald, became an avid scholar. "I already feel the benificial effects of the Govr. & McTavish's marriages — she has picked up sense enough to infer from their having changed partners, that the old ones were defficient in learning," wrote her husband, Archie. Frances's stay at Red River may have been brief, but her influence was profound. "Mrs. Simpson's presence here makes a change in us," said Simpson's old fellow traveller James Macmillan. It was a sentiment that reverberated throughout Rupert's Land and changed the way his officers looked at marriage under Simpson's governance.

George Simpson had eleven children by his five wives. Only four of them have descendants to the present. From them, some six hundred descendants now reside in Canada, the United States, the United Kingdom, and Australia.

Sir GEORGE SIMPSON (1792-1860)
m. MARIA (Simpson)
m. ELIZABETH SINCLAIR (1804–1878)
m. JANE KLYNE (1808–1879)
m. MARGARET TAYLOR (1810–1885)
m. FRANCES R. SIMPSON (1812–1853)

— MARIA LOUISA SIMPSON (1815–1891)
m. DONALD MACTAVISH (1796–1849)
m. DONALD CAMPBELL (1808–1892)

— GEORGE S. MCTAVISH (1834–1895)
m. Mrs. George McTavish (d. bef1867)
m. EMILY MOORE (1847–1886)
— JANE M.MCTAVISH (1836–1934)
m. JAMES THORBURN (1830–1905)
— JOHN HENRY MCTAVISH (1838–1888)
m. MARIA ROWAND (1849–1889)
— DONALD C. MCTAVISH (1844–1913)
m. LYDIA C. CHRISTIE (1853–1886)
— MARIA L. MCTAVISH (1846–1918)
m. MATTHEW S. BEESTON (1857–1931)
— MARY MCTAVISH (1847–1932)

— ISABELLA SIMPSON (1819–1842)
m. JOHN COOK GORDON (1803–1853)

— THEODORE COOK GORDON (b. 1840)
— (son) GORDON (b. 1842)

— MARIA SIMPSON (1822–1838)
m. ROBERT WALLACE (d. 1838)

— no descendants

— JAMES KEITH SIMPSON (1825–1901)
m. CATHERINE MOIGNON (1831–aft1901)

— no descendants

— GEORGE S.SIMPSON (1827–1894)
m. ISABELLA YALE (1840–1927)

— GEORGE F. SIMPSON (1858–1926)
m. SHIRLEY V. LEIGH (1865–1945)
— ELIZA A. SIMPSON (1865–1872)
— MILES YALE SIMPSON (1870–1887)
— JAMES YALE SIMPSON (1872–1898)
— MINNIE SIMPSON (1874–1874)

— JOHN M. SIMPSON (1829–1900)
m. AMELIA FIDLER (1839–1900)

— CHARLES SIMPSON (1860–1957)
m. ADELINE DENIG (1857–1932)
m. WINIFRED LEGARY
— JOHN SIMPSON (1861–1885)
— ALFRED SIMPSON (1864–1890)
— GEORGE SIMPSON (1866–aft1901)
— MARGARET ANN SIMPSON (1868–1942)
m. ZACHERIA LILLIE (b. 1866)
— THOMAS A. SIMPSON (1871–1964)
m. ANNIE (Sarah) OLSEN (b. 1873)
— BENJAMIN SIMPSON (1874–1960)
m. CATHERINE DUCHARME (1887–1966)
— DAVID JAMES SIMPSON (1876–1926)
m. VIRGINIE MORIN (1875–1908)
— WILLIAM R. SIMPSON (1878–1908)
— MARY SOPHIA SIMPSON (1833–1925)
m. ROBERT ABBOTT (1874–1948)

— GEORGE G. SIMPSON (1831–1832)

— no descendants

— FRANCES W. SIMPSON (1833–1881)
m. ANGUS CAMERON (1823–1864)
m. EDWARD F. HODDER (1836–1915)

— GEORGE S. CAMERON (1857–1858)
— ANGUS F. CAMERON (1859–1863)
— ELIZABETH CAMERON (1861–1883)
— ANNIE HODDER CAMERON (1863–1864)

— AUGUSTA D.SIMPSON (1841–1888)

— no descendants

— MARGARET M. SIMPSON (1843–1871)
m. ALEXANDER D. GORDON (1830–1863)
m. JAMES BUTLER-HUGHES (1825–1871)

— ALEXANDER H. GORDON (1864–1892)
m. MARY ADELL ARD (1866–1952)
— A. BUTLER-HUGHES (1865–1918)
m. ARTHUR OWEN (1862–1917)
— HELEN BUTLER-HUGHES (1867–1886)
— NORA GEORGINA HUGHES (1869–1869)

— JOHN HENRY SIMPSON (1850–1898)
m. MARY SCOTT (1843-1930)

— no descendants

7

"Character Book": The Strangest Man I Ever Knew

*Simpson showed in his Book of Servant's
Characters as a leader who retained the power
to command by reason of a profound
understanding of men.*
— *Douglas MacKay*

By the early 1830s Simpson was beginning to suffer a mysterious ailment that was to strike him periodically throughout the rest of his life and which would eventually cause his death. During Simpson's lifetime it went by several names — apoplexy, syncope, and epilepsy — all ill-defined terms for some kind of neurological impairment. But what the express nature of that impairment was in Simpson's case has never been satisfactorily explained. Whatever it was, its manifestation was a sudden fainting or seizure with collapse and unconsciousness for a period of time, followed by apparent complete recovery.

Meanwhile, in his private life, George must have felt like a bear in a cage. For ten years he had coursed the rivers and crossed the mountains and run the cascades, and by his own words was never happier than when doing so. In winter he had made gruelling rounds of inspection of his posts. He was a traveller by temperament and preference, and the simple fact of marriage was bound to constrain his life, and he wasn't prepared for it. Now he was confined to "4 rooms and a kitchen" and he became irritable. He spent much of his time fighting with the cook and her servant husband. The cook lavished devotion on Frances, but constantly drew "odious comparisons between her present situation & that which she held for ten years at Grove House."

Just as if he were on the trail, Simpson tried "Damning and Bitching" her, and even a "Dish of Billingsgate." But it turned out she could be as rancorous as Simpson. She "beats me hollow," Simpson complained, "and makes the whole fort ring…. The very look of me now throws her into a fever."

Her husband was the manservant in the establishment, good enough at his job when sober, but he too often "washed his throat" with rum until Simpson "gave him such a pounding as made his Bones ache for a month, which has cured him."

In this depressing atmosphere, Simpson sat down to a strange pastime. He would write character sketches of every one of his chief factors, chief traders, clerks, and postmasters throughout the entire fur-trade system. It would be a tour de force to write a personal note on every single one of the officers under his command. Some had been thorns in his side from the beginning. Some had never quite caught on to the system of economy and regularity. Most had been around since the old fur war days, and were hardly men to find their proper place in the new scheme of things. And some, of course, had become lazy, or licentious, or drunken, or pompous, or less than totally honest, or old, or fat.

And some of the men considered in the "Character Book" — and this is often forgotten — met with Simpson's entire approval.

The entries would be for his eyes alone, completely secret. No one would ever read them but him. Simpson would only number each entry, and on a separate sheet of paper he would keep the key to the numbers. And the whole would be kept under lock and key, kept hidden for the rest of his life.

This is Simpson, then, in his private never-to-be-shared moments of reflection. It is Simpson, laid bare.

Simpson begins with two men for whom his deep personal dislike seasoned his assessments, the first a man whose pomposity had irked him for years:

> Colin Robertson, a frothy trifling conceited man, who would starve in any other Country and is perfectly useless here: fancies, or rather attempts to pass himself off as a clever fellow, a man of taste, of talents and of refinement; to none of which I need scarcely say he has the slightest pretension.

There — he had that off his chest. But Robertson had recently bungled the winter road to Norway House, had wasted the budget, destroyed provisions, and left furs abandoned in the woods through neglect and mismanagement. Simpson had some recent grounds for his discontent with this man.

Similarly, his old nemesis from the Athabasca days receives no praise:

> John Clarke, a boasting, ignorant low fellow who rarely speaks the truth and is strongly suspected of dishonesty; his commanding appearance & pompous manner, however, give him a good deal of influence over Indians and Servants; and his total want of every principle or feeling, allied to fair dealing, honour & integrity, together with his cruel and Tyrannical disposition render him eminently qualified for playing the lawless, cold-blooded Bravo in opposition. He is in short a disgrace to the Fur Trade.

In Clarke's case there was some truth to Simpson's harsh judgment, as Clarke had recently been caught in shady speculation of Company property for personal gain.

Alexander Stewart comes off with flying colours, except that "'tis strongly suspected [he] is given to tippling in private." His old friend John George McTavish, unfortunately, "has of late Years become very heavy unwieldy and inactive." However, George Keith, who opposed Simpson in the Athabasca, was "a man of highly correct conduct and Character and much attention to his business; well Educated and respectfully connected: Not wanting in personal courage when pushed altho' rather timid, nervous and indecisive on ordinary occasions."

His brother, James Keith, is likewise "the most faultless member of the Fur Trade." J.D. [John Dugald] Cameron is "Strictly correct in all his conduct and dealings." John Charles is a man of "veracity and integrity," but "so irritable and violent at times that 'tis feared he will someday get into trouble." Edward Smith is praised for his "business which is managed with regularity and œconomy." Joseph Beioley is "A steady well conducted little man whose word can be depended upon."

But Angus Bethune* is described as

> [a] very poor creature, vain, self sufficient and trifling, who makes his own comfort his principal study; possessing little Nerve and no decision in anything: of a snarling vindictive disposition, and neither liked nor respected by his associates, Servants or Indians. His Services would be overpaid by the victuals himself & Family consume.

But Simpson heaps praise on Alexander Christie:

> This is one of our best characters, an honourable, correct, upright good hearted man as can be found in any Country; beloved & respected by all who know him, attentive to business, qualified to be useful in any branch thereof and a valuable member of the concern.

Simpson was utterly baffled by William McIntosh's success as a chief factor:

> A revengeful cold blooded black hearted Man whom I consider capable of anything that is bad: possessing no abilities beyond such as

---

* Angus Bethune was the ancestor of Dr. Norman Bethune, of twentieth-century fame.

qualify him to cheat an unfortunate Indian and
to be guilty of a mean dirty trick: Suspicious,
Cruel & Tyrannical without honour or integrity,
in short, I have never been able to discover one
good trait in his character.

On the other hand, perhaps of all the men of the fur trade,
Simpson had the greatest admiration for John Rowand, Chief
Factor in charge of the Edmonton District. Short, weighing some
three hundred pounds, Rowand was rowdy, uncouth, kind, and
generous, and the best fur trader in the system, and Simpson
loved him:

> John Rowand: One of the most pushing bustling
> Men in the Service whose zeal and ambition in
> the discharge of his duties is unequalled, ren-
> dering him totally regardless of every personal
> Comfort and indulgence. Warm hearted and
> Friendly in an extraordinary degree where he
> has a liking, but on the contrary his prejudices
> exceedingly strong.... An excellent Trader who
> has the peculiar talent of attracting the fiercest
> Indians to him while he rules them with a Rod
> of Iron and so daring that he beards their Chiefs
> in the open camp while surrounded by their
> Warriors; has likewise a Wonderful influence
> over his people. Has by his superior manage-
> ment realized more money for the concern than
> any three of his Colleagues since the Coalition;
> and altho' his Education has been defective is a
> very clear headed clever fellow. Will not tell a

> lie (which is very uncommon in this Country)
> but has sufficient address to evade the truth
> when it suits his purpose: full of drollery and
> humour and generally liked and respected by
> Indians Servants and his own equals.

Peter Warren Dease is likewise a man whose "judgement is sound, his manners are more pleasing and easy than those of many of his Colleagues, and altho' not calculated to make a shining figure may be considered a very respectable Member of the Concern."

When Simpson was looking for an officer to oversee his reforms on the Columbia, his choice fell on John McLoughlin. However, McLoughlin was a strange fellow, with latent energies tending toward the violent. Standing well over six feet, he was, wrote Simpson,

> A very bustling active man who can go through
> a great deal of business but is wanting in system
> and regularity, and has not the talent of manag-
> ing the few associates & clerks under his author-
> ity: has a good deal of influence with Indians and
> speaks Siaulteaux tolerably well. Very Zealous
> in the discharge of his public duties and a man
> of strict honour and integrity but a great stick-
> ler for rights and priviledges and sets himself up
> for a righter of Wrongs. Very anxious to obtain
> a lead among his colleagues with whom he has
> not much influence owing to his ungovernable
> Violent temper and turbulent disposition, and
> would be a troublesome man to the Compy if

he had sufficient influence to form and tact to
manage a party, in short, would be a Radical
in any country — under any Government and
under any circumstances; and if he had not
pacific people to deal with, would be eternally
embroiled in "affairs of honor" on the merest
trifle arising. I conceive from the irritability of
his temper more than a quarrelsome disposition. Altogether a disagreeable man to do business with as it is impossible to go with him in
all things and a difference of opinion almost
amounts to a declaration of hostilities, yet a
good hearted man and a pleasant companion.

Of all Simpson's biographical sketches in the "Character
Book," this one was the most personal, most frustrating and irri-
tating of them all — and the most prophetic. He had handpicked
McLoughlin for the superintendency of the Columbia, and no
one has ever faulted McLoughlin for the sincerity of his work.
Simpson had twice been to the Columbia to oversee McLoughlin's
work, and now, three years after the last visit, Simpson's temper
still bristles, still rankles and frustrates. He cannot understand
how McLoughlin manages to hold together his leadership on
the Columbia despite his lack of system and regularity. He rec-
ognizes the radical in McLoughlin, that only his disorganization
prevents him from being a dangerous man. Simpson's biography
vents all of this frustration, and yet in the end his heart warms to
one who can at the same time be so good-hearted and a pleasant
companion. Yet in the end McLoughlin's career will end on his
pathetic attempt to set himself up as a righter of wrongs in the
case of his son's death, as Simpson predicted.

Of those officers who were to rise highest in the Company, Duncan Finlayson was to surpass them all, and Simpson speaks of him in superlatives: "a highly upright honourable correct man of good Education and superior abilities…. Much liked by his Equals, inferiors and natives…. Firm Cool and decisive, one of our best Legislators and most effective practical Men, and his private conduct & character are models worthy of imitation; in short, he may be ranked high among the most respectable and efficient men of his class." Finlayson married Isobel, the sister of Lady Frances, became one of the best governors of Assiniboia, Simpson's right-hand man at Lachine, guardian to his children, and one of his executors. On his retirement he was admitted as a member of the Committee in London.

When Simpson came to consider his men of second class — that is, chief traders — he did so with a specific consideration in mind: were they suitable for promotion to the rank of chief factor? His attention therefore narrows to that specific object. This was important to Simpson, because such men would then sit on council and have a voice in proceedings. And he would have to rely on them in his great network of empire.

Of the twenty-five men at the rank of chief trader, Simpson fully approved of seven. Some he has utter contempt for, and in some, like John Work, he seems bemused by their peculiarities, even while conceding their head for business:

> John Work. About 45 Years of Age. A very steady pains taking Man, regular, œconomical and attentive in business, and bears a fair private character. Has been a useful man for many years

and must always be so from his persevering and steady and regular habits. A queer looking fellow, of Clownish Manners and address, indeed there is a good deal of simplicity approaching to idiocy in his appearance, he is nevertheless a Shrewd Sensible Man, and not deficient in firmness when necessary; was bred an operative farmer.

Work's appearance did not improve with age. Years later, with half his upper lip cut away to remove a lesion, he was "a queer looking chap, of his hair there remains but three small elf locks which protrude far between over his Coat neck, and the point of his nose is actually coming in contact with that of his chin."

Yet despite his clownish appearance, Work had a long and distinguished career with the HBC, becoming in the end a member of the board of management for the Company's affairs with Alexander Grant Dallas, who was to become Simpson's successor as governor-in-chief.

John Harriott comes off with flying colours:

A finished Trader. Speaks Cree like a Native and is a great favourite with Indians: has much influence likewise with the people and is generally esteemed by his colleagues. Strong, active, and fit for Severe duty. Mild tempered, well disposed, and bears an excellent private character.

On the contrary, Alexander McTavish is "a sly, smerking, plausible fellow who lies habitually, full of low cunning, suspicion and intrigue ... lays claim to a wonderful degree of foresight and exhibits a vast deal of after wisdom, finds fault with every thing and every body with a view to persuade others that he would improve upon the existing state of affairs if he had a voice in the management; but that, he is not likely to have."

Robert Miles, who had been so useful to Simpson in the Athabasca, while still "the best Clerk in the Country as regards Penmanship and Knowledge of accounts," has nevertheless become "devoted to his pot and his pipe.... Full of childish jealousy and ridiculously stiff and stately behind his Desk as also behind his pipe, in short a wiseacre who would in England be a Pot House Politician."

He noted that John Siveright "shot a man in cold blood many years ago and ... is still looked upon as a Murderer." Simpson has no fault with Cuthbert Cumming, describing him as "a very fit man to come forward." Alexander McLeod would have made "an excellent *Guide* altho' he adds little respectability to the 'Fur Trade' as a 'Partner.'" Alexander Fisher is "a habitual liar without conduct or principal, and was becoming so much addicted to Liquor that I found it necessary to remove him a few years ago to one of our most Sober stations."

Certainly Simpson was not disappointed in all of his chief traders. Archibald McDonald, for instance, was described as a "shrewd, clear headed Man who Studies his own interest in all things, obsequious in courting favour, but would be overbearing in power." Nevertheless, Simpson concludes, he "would make a better figure on our Council board than many of his colleagues or even than the majority of those now seated there."

But of the men who stand in the "Character Book" locked in time, two of the chief traders have achieved a greater fame. These are Samuel Black, who had opposed Simpson during the Athabasca campaign, and Peter Skene Ogden.

Before the union, Black was renowned in the Indian country as the "most outrageous of the North West bullies," a "young man without a shadow of self respect in his make up." So questionable were his tactics that even the old Nor'westers did not want him in the new concern, and he was excluded from the Deed Poll in 1821. But this was not Simpson's way. In 1823, on the argument that Black and Ogden were "instruments rather than contrivers of mischief," both were invited back into the fold.

Black was later described as "a splendid example of the metamorphosis of even the more violent Nor'Westers." But Simpson was not fooled by the propensities of this child of darkness. In 1832 he described him thus:

> Samuel Black. About 52 Years of Age. The strangest man I ever knew. So wary & suspicious that it is scarcely possible to get a direct answer from him on any point, and when he does speak or write on any subject so prolix that it is quite fatiguing to attempt following him. A perfectly honest man and his generosity might be considered indicative of a warmth of heart if he was not known to be a cold blooded fellow who could be guilty of any Cruelty and would be a perfect Tyrant if he had power. Can never forget what he may consider a slight or insult, and fancies that every man has a design upon him. Very cool, resolute to desperation, and equal to the cutting of a throat with perfect deliberation: yet his word when he can be brought to the point may be depended on. A Don Quixote in appearance, Ghastly, raw

boned and lanthorn jawed, yet strong vigorous
and active. Has not the talent of conciliating
Indians by whom he is disliked, but who are
ever in dread of him, and well they may be so,
as he is ever on his guard against them and so
suspicious that offensive and defensive preparation seem to be the study of his Life, having
Dirks, Knives and Loaded Pistols concealed
about his Person and in all directions about
his Establishment even under his Table cloth
at meals and in his Bed. He would be admirably adapted for the Service of the North West
coast where the Natives are so treacherous were
it not that he cannot agree with his colleagues
which renders it necessary to give him a distinct charge. I should be sorry to see a man of
such character at our Council board. Tolerably
well Educated and most patient and laborious
in whatever he sets about, but so tedious that it
is impossible to get through business with him.

The distinct charge that Simpson found for him was in an
exploration of the sources of the Finley and Stikine rivers in
1824, in which Black distinguished himself, and largely restored
his reputation.

In the end, Black was a victim of his own propensities.
He could not handle the Natives. He was the direct cause of
the deaths of four traders at the hands of the Beaver Indians
on the Peace River, when it appears Black was guilty of "wife-
lifting." His colleague Donald Manson warned Simpson: "It
was no uncommon thing for the Indians to draw their knives

[on Black]." The whole matter caught up with Black in 1841. In charge of the Thompson River post, he was shot in the back by a disgruntled Native.

Peter Skene Ogden, like Samuel Black, had been excluded from the Union but brought back in to stay under Simpson's control. Simpson's assessment in the "Character Book" cuts closest to the core of Ogden's being — a sly, crafty, devil of a man capable of the most sinister acts:

> Peter Skene Ogden. About 45 Years of Age. A keen, sharp off hand fellow of superior abilities to most of his colleagues, very hardy and active and not sparing of his personal labour.... Has been very Wild & thoughtless and is still fond of coarse practical jokes, but with all the appearances of thoughtlessness he is a very cool calculating fellow who is capable of doing any thing to gain his own ends.... I consider him one of the most unprincipled Men in the Indian Country, who would soon get into habits of dissipation if he were not restrained by the fear of these operating against his interests, and if he does indulge in that way, madness to which he has a predisposition, will follow as a matter of course.

If Black was the bludgeon, Ogden was the rapier. Black struck with the stick, Ogden pricked with the knife. That was their distinctive natures. And so Simpson sent Black into the solitary wilderness of northern New Caledonia, while Ogden was sent to confront the Americans of the southern frontier. He needed this cunning man who could harass with craft, without creating an international incident.

Simpson knew that future promotions would come from the long list of clerks under his command, and his purpose was to note those who might in future be recommended to greater responsibility.

His cousin Thomas Simpson, with his university background, "is hardy & active and will in due time if he goes on as he promises be one of the most complete men of business in the Country." Thomas's brother Alexander, likewise, is described as "correct in conduct and private character & promises to be a valuable man in the Service."

His personal manservant for ten years, Thomas Taylor — the brother of Simpson's wife, Margaret Taylor — has "been one of the most effective Postmasters in the Country.... Is a great favourite with Indians, is 'a Jack of all Trades' and altogether a very useful man."

Thomas Dears is "a flippant, superficial, trifling creature — who lies more frequently than he speaks the truth, can take a Glass of Grog and I strongly suspect is given to pilfering." Erland Erlandson, a Dane in the world of Scotsmen and Métis, "entered the Service as a labourer from one of the Prison Ships at Chatham where he was a Prisoner of War." Francis Ermatinger, it seems, had "got into disgrace lately in consequence of having employed one of the Company's Servants in cutting off the Ears of an Indian who had an intrigue with his Woman, but which would not have been thought so much of, had it been done by himself in the heat of passion or as a punishment for Horse Stealing." Charles McKenzie was a "queer-prosing long-winded little highland body, who traces his lineage back to Ossian and claims the Laureateship of Albany District." Métis Thomas

McKay "is known to every Indian ... and his name is a host of Strength carrying terror with it as he has sent many of them to their 'long home.'" Timid Charles Ross was "a good classical scholar and a man of very correct conduct but so nervous at times it is quite painful to see him." Charles Bouc was "useful as a drudge." William Cowie had been "shamefully inveigled ... into an injudicious Marriage with a half breed Girl." George Delormier's only saving grace was that he "walks well on Snow Shoes." And Thomas Frazer, to Simpson's pleasant surprise, "has saved about £4,000 ... which to a man in his Walk of Life is a fortune."

But of all the clerks under Simpson's observation, one was to rise far above the station of the others, and Simpson recognized his abilities from the beginning. That was James Douglas:

> A stout powerful active Man of good conduct and respectable abilities: tolerably well Educated, expresses himself clearly on paper, understands our Counting House business and is an excellent Trader. Well qualified for any Service requiring bodily exertion, firmness of mind and the exercise of Sound judgement, but furiously violent when roused. Has every reason to look forward to early promotion and is a likely man to fill a place at our Council board in course of time. Stationed in the Columbia Deptmnt.

In the course of time James Douglas rose to the highest positions in the HBC, became governor of the colonies of Vancouver Island and British Columbia, and received the accolade of knighthood in 1863.

In a sense, Douglas was McLoughlin's alter ego. A great-hearted man, he possessed ideals without McLoughlin's vision; he kept books correctly, where McLoughlin merely kept busy; where McLoughlin was violent, Douglas could be coolly murderous. Unlike McLoughlin, Douglas had no qualms about abandoning Fort Vancouver in favour of Fort Victoria, if that was the decision of the Company. In many ways he was the perfect foil to McLoughlin. If Simpson was confounded at how McLoughlin managed to maintain order on the Columbia, much of that order was surely due to Douglas's steady hand. Douglas picked up the work of McLoughlin after 1845, and to his leadership must be accounted much of the success in keeping Vancouver Island and the mainland under British control, and eventually part of Canada.

Thus, Simpson's appointment of McLoughlin, and McLoughlin's appointment of Douglas were propitious, securing, as in fact it did, the Pacific Coast for the later Dominion of Canada.

And so it went, through a long list of 156 chief factors, chief traders, clerks, and postmasters. Nowhere else in fur-trade literature can such a treasure of mini biographies be found. Men who would now be nothing but names on a list of Company servants stand for a moment in the light of history as real people, each with his own peculiarity, virtue, or foible. We can be thankful that Simpson's preoccupied mind in the winter of 1832 found time for this diversion.

Simpson's judgments, it has been pointed out, were not always flawless, and were sometimes motivated by long-suffering personal dislike, but they offer a penetrating look at the men Simpson had to work with, and at Simpson himself.

The "Character Book" of George Simpson stands as a grand summary of the men of the fur trade. Historian E.E. Rich summed it up cogently: "It is impossible to read through Simpson's 'Character Book' without being overwhelmed by the shrewd and caustic comment. This was a revelation of uncompromising knowledge and capacity." The historian Douglas MacKay looked upon the "Character Book" as evidence of Simpson's "power to command by reason of a profound understanding of men."

8

Diplomacy:
As If Awakened from a Dream

*Sir George Simpson did not only see far ahead.
He had the more serviceable quality of putting
great ideas into practice.*

— *Charles V. Sale*

Following his return from London in 1834, three problems faced
Simpson. First, law and order within Rupert's Land; second,
parts of the Arctic still required exploration; third, the Russians
were an ongoing pain in the side of empire on the northwest
coast of North America. Simpson would deal with all of them.

By 1835 the HBC repurchased the colony of Assiniboia,
which it had sold to the Earl of Selkirk in 1811. Simpson had to
turn his mind to the rule of law in Rupert's Land, and whether
his audience was London or Rupert's Land, Simpson played the
role of lawmaker brilliantly.

He established a law without judges, without codes of law, without lawyers, and without police. Improbable as that may seem, with minor modifications it was a system ideally suited to the settlers of Red River and Rupert's Land, and it lasted until confederation.

Simpson established the Council of Assiniboia as the chief judiciary body in Assiniboia. It would have as its head, not a judge, but a recorder, a concept borrowed from English municipal law, whose duty it was to convene the courts and record the proceedings. Assiniboia was divided into judicial divisions that varied in number over the years, each with appointed magistrates, who also varied in number from time to time. Judgments would be rendered by a jury of peers, whose number could be less than twelve if that number of tried and true men could not be found. The council sat as a "General Quarterly" to hear appeal cases or crimes of a more serious nature.

Simpson combined military and policing duties into one body, a Volunteer Corps, of seventy members. Enlisted men served both as privates in a military corps and as police officers in their communities — a police force on a military model. Their duties included both protecting against external danger and providing internal police security. In time, there being no external dangers and little need for such a large band of police officers, the force was reduced to a fifteen-man constabulary.

This was justice the citizens of Red River could understand. But the members of the Select Committee of 1857 could not. Simpson explained it to them in simple terms:

> Q1173: There is no legislative power at all, as I understand; there is no power to make laws in any body?
> **Simpson:** We make such laws as are necessary.

Q1174: Do you make Statutes at all?
Simpson: No.

Q1172: Do you make Ordinances?
Simpson: No, we have never had an occasion to make ordinances; we have passed certain Resolutions of Council.

Q1157: What little [law enforcement] is to be done he [the Recorder] does?
Simpson: Yes; our gaols [jails] are almost always empty; they scarcely ever have an inmate.

Q1296: Then, in short, they [the settlers at Red River] may not be aware of the laws and regulations under which they are living?
Simpson: The laws and regulations are so very few that they know them perfectly.

Q 1394: And that you call administering justice in that country:
Simpson: Yes.

Q1395: We may take that as a specimen of the administration of justice in those countries under the rule of the Hudson's Bay Company?
Simpson: Of the absence of crime, I should hope; we claim to ourselves great credit.

Laws so few the people knew them perfectly: no statutes, no ordinances, no crime, the jails empty, the citizens law-abiding.

It was more than the legislators could fathom. But it was a system perfectly suited to the lives of the settlers. Later, the diarist Alexander Begg could write of the legal system brought to them by George Simpson: "Our laws as administered savored more of arbitration than law and in that respect suited our requirements better than if a pack of lawyers had been amongst us urging us with all the quibbles best known to them to eat each other up in useless suits." Nothing could sum up the Simpson system more succinctly.

In 1835 Simpson decided on an ambitious plan to survey, under HBC auspices, the entire Arctic coast that had not yet been explored. This involved all unexplored territory from Cape Barrow in northern Alaska in the west, to Fury and Hecla Strait in the east, a distance of some 72 degrees of latitude. About 41 degrees of this had already been surveyed by the two Franklin expeditions, but most of it would have to be traversed again to reach the unexplored coasts. This amounted to roughly 1,600 miles in a straight line.

For the first phase, Simpson picked a likely candidate for Arctic exploration. This was Peter Warren Dease, a Company factor who had been attached to the Franklin Expedition as provisions officer. He was experienced, steady, and reliable.

Simpson needed a young co-leader who might be expected to show dash and initiative, take chances, and do the unexpected. He picked Thomas Simpson, his energetic but mercurial cousin. The Dease-Simpson Arctic Expedition spent three years in the polar region. Under extreme difficulties at times, the men pressed forward toward their goals. In the end, the instructions set by George Simpson were not only met, but exceeded.

In 1837 the men travelled down the Mackenzie River and westward to Point Barrow, the northernmost point in Alaska.

This closed the western gap of exploration. In 1838 the men explored eastward, but found Coronation Gulf blocked with ice. This brought out the best in Thomas Simpson. With a small crew, he walked along the shore. His discoveries were a tour de force. In a few days he had discovered Dease Strait, Victoria Island, Queen Maud Gulf, an extra thirty miles of the North American coastline, and the entrance to Victoria Strait. That exploration stands as one of the great accomplishments of Arctic discovery, but it was to be dwarfed by the successes of the same men in 1839.

While the summer of 1838 found Coronation Gulf and Dease Strait choked with ice, in 1839 the explorers found an open sea. In a rapid thrust to the east, they found, unexpectedly, that the continent did not join with King William Land, but that instead a strait, later called Simpson Strait, led eastward to Chantrey Inlet. The goals of the expedition had been accomplished. But Thomas was not satisfied. He insisted that the men continue eastward to see whether a strait did in fact exist separating Boothia from the mainland and providing a waterway into the Gulf of Boothia.

The party crossed Chantrey Inlet and found the land trending in a northeasterly direction. Forty miles on, the expedition was brought to a halt by prevailing winds that made further progress impossible. The Boothia question, it seemed, would not be resolved on this expedition. Now Simpson and Dease went inland to a small rise of the ground, and looked through the windy haze, peering in deepest concentration to the east. There they saw, or thought they saw, a marvellous sight:

> Far without lay several lofty islands; and in the northeast, more distant still, appeared some high blue land. This, which we designated

Cape Sir John Ross, is in all probability one of
the southeastern promontories of Boothia. We
could therefore hardly doubt being now arrived
at that large gulph, uniformly described by the
Esquimeaux as containing many islands, and,
with numerous indentations, running down
to the southward till it approaches within forty
miles of Repulse and Wager Bays.

Mirages are common in deserts such as the barren north-
lands. It is one of the great tragedies of northern exploration that
what the men thought they saw was not there at all. They weren't
looking at an open sea, but eighty miles of solid rock. Boothia
was a peninsula, not an island, and the failure to recognize that
fact was to bring great tragedy to Thomas Simpson.

The success of the Dease-Simpson Expedition brought
fame to the HBC. John Henry Pelly, Governor of the London
Committee, was awarded a baronetcy, and George Simpson a
knighthood. Peter Warren Dease and Thomas Simpson were
awarded pensions.

But the very success of the expedition brought tragedy to
Thomas Simpson. The next summer, while travelling through
Dakota territory in the United States, he went mad. Thinking
that his two travelling companions were going to kill him in the
night to steal his "secret" of a North West Passage, he made a
preemptive strike, murdered both men in the night, then blew
off the top of his own head.

Since 1824, Simpson had planned to drive the American trading
ships from the north Pacific and take over trade with the Russian

American Company (RAC) in Alaska. In this he had been successful, and now, in 1838, he was about to complete his work with an agreement with the Russian America Company.

On June 17, 1838, Simpson left his home at 5 Trinity Square, hard by the Tower of London, and boarded the steamship *Britannia*, where Governor Pelly and his family were already awaiting him. In Hamburg he embarked on a series of business calls, social calls, parties, dinner engagements, and sightseeing. From Hamburg the party travelled to Christiana (modern Oslo), Stockholm, Helsinki, and Russia. At St. Petersburg his passport and pistols were taken into custody by the port authorities. Simpson wrote: "[When I] saw an Officer take a fancy to mine I asked for acknowledgement of them for which I was refused. I therefore addressed a letter to the Collector intimating the delivery of Arms and begging they might be returned on departure."

Getting down to the business at hand of attempting an agreement with the Russian American Company, Simpson visited the British Chargé d'Affaires, but found him to be a "flippant, smirking, smart-looking man" who offered no hope of a settlement with the Russians. He met with the bankers of the Russian American Company and learned that "dividends were 14p. Cent every 2 Years or 7p. Cent. Anm." Simpson was beginning to collect information necessary for an agreement. He visited the fur warehouses to inspect the quality of the Russian furs. On July 30 he met a gentleman by the name of Baron Stenglozh, who promised to provide letters of introduction to the directors, who later "said they would be happy to give favourable consideration to my [Simpson's] proposition."

After some more sightseeing, Simpson arrived at the Russian American House, where, for the first time, he met Baron Wrangel, his counterpart in the RAC. Simpson described him as "an extraordinary looking, ferret Eyed, Red Whiskered & mustachioed little creature; in full Regimentals & not half the size of [Chief Factor Joseph] Beioley, very thin weak & delicate, but evidently a sharp, clever little creature."

Never mind the appearances, here was the man Simpson had been waiting to do business with: "Wrangel seems to have a controuling power, in short he seems to have the principal management and I imagine represents the Government in their councils." The Baron, instead of talking obstacles, immediately expressed his opinion that "they would be most happy to establish a good understanding in the H.B. Coy." Nevertheless, after Wrangel mentioned at random a number of obstacles to agreement, Simpson adds, "the impression on my mind is that they will not have any dealing with us."

The business with the Russians proceeded slowly, without any conclusive agreement. Simpson had by now zeroed in on the one person to deal with: "Wrangel & I very thick. A nice intelligent, clever little man, regret much we have not seen much of each other. To call tomorrow."

Wrangel's call the next day, Friday September 17, 1838, brought an agreement between the two men almost effortlessly. Simpson described how it happened:

> At 11 Baron Wrangal entered [and] we spoke much about arrangements. Friendly intercourse … had nearly separated when I in a last effort threw out another Bait … that of Selling them our Fort Simpson Furs which they could import as the produce of their own Colony on the N.W. Coast & thereby be admissable to entry for Home Consumption or Sale to the Chinese free

of Duty. This threw a new light on the subject. The little Baron opened his Eyes as if wakened from a Dream [and] caught at the thing instantly. I pointed out to him that it would not be worth our while to enter into any partial arrangements with the Russian American Coy. nor to have any dealings with people who would descend to the Splitting of Straws, but if they would take all we had to propose as a whole & entered into a liberal & Friendly compact with us it would be greatly to their advantage & enable them to double their Dividends very soon.

Having delivered the carrot, Simpson laid on the stick:

On the contrary, we should have nothing to do with them but in determined opposition & that in 2 or 3 years hence the consequence would be that instead of paying 14 p. Cent every second year they would pay no more than 7 every second year.

And there you have it — Simpson collecting bits of information here and there, then offering a deal too good — indeed too dangerous — to turn down.

His business with Wrangel done, Simpson simply "wrote to the directors a formal letter declining their counter proposition referring them to our conversation with Wrangal."

In this, Simpson had shown himself to be a consummate negotiator, friendly and approachable during negotiations, but tough as nails at the close.

There was little left to do in Russia. Simpson had wrapped up the matter and reached an agreement in principal in a meeting with Wrangel that could not have taken more than an hour to complete. On September 15 he left Russia, "tired of its Govt. Laws institutions &c." Simpson wrote: "[at] 8 in the evening the Villainous Customs and Police officers took their departure, good riddence... [and] at 6 A.M. Got our Steam up Weighed Anchor and off."

And, of course, before setting sail, Simpson received back the pistols that were taken from him on arrival.

In 1839, Simpson travelled back to Hamburg, where he met Wrangel to sign the agreement that would guarantee peace between the HBC and the Russian American Company. So solid was this agreement that many years later, when he met with the Select Committee in 1857, Simpson could put on record that during the Crimean War between England and Russia, an agreement was made whereby the two fur companies would not interfere with each other's trade during hostilities, that the Russian and English governments both confirmed the arrangement, even during wartime, and that the agreement "was strictly observed during the whole war."

Simpson was now master of his realm. In 1839 the Committee at last gave him the title of governor-in-chief, though he had in fact held that position since 1826. The government in London had given notice that it intended to elevate Simpson to a knighthood. And in Rupert's Land his officers sought an opportunity to put on record once more, as they had done in 1825, their complete confidence in their leader:

The unexampled prosperity of the British fur trade during a period of nearly twenty years under the direction of Governor Simpson, to whose masterly arrangements that prosperity is mostly owing, has called forth the admiration of every person interested in its affairs, while that gentleman's active habits of business, conciliating disposition and address have been productive in the happiest effects in diffusing a spirit of enterprise and harmonious cooperation throughout the wilds of British North America unequalled perhaps in any other part of the world.

Simpson had the approbation of his world. Now he could indulge in one final long-held wish — to travel around the world. That would be his next adventure.

9

Rupert's Land:
Everything Is in Extremes

*Pen and ink sketch
of George Simpson
by Sir James
Alexander Grant.*

Looking at the pen sketch of Simpson made in 1841 by Sir James Alexander Grant, with his immaculately groomed, carefully manicured, and well-fed city look, we can easily see what Letitia Hargrave saw when she met Simpson in London in 1840: "a good-natured, happy-looking, dumpy man." But from the same sketch we can scarcely imagine what Lieutenant Henry Lefroy saw in 1843, when he described him as "the toughest looking old fellow I ever saw, built upon the Egyptian model, height two diameters, or like one of those short, square, massy pillars one sees in our old country church. He is a fellow whom nothing will kill." Letitia saw the man of the drawing room and the salon; Lefroy saw the man on the trail. They were as different as night and day.

It must have been an exhilarating day, that chilly January of 1841, when Governor George Simpson headed to Buckingham Palace. He was going to see the queen — the young queen, the new queen, only four years on the throne, only twenty-two years of age, petite and pretty, the name Victoria not yet synonymous with one of the great ages in history. For Simpson it was the culmination of an unremitting twenty years of labour in the service of the Company, Country, and Empire. Young Queen Victoria bestowed on George Simpson the accolade of a knighthood. From that day, January 25, 1841, Mr. George Simpson would be known to history as Sir George Simpson.

On the third of March 1841, Simpson started from London to fulfill a long-held ambition — to journey around the world and to write about it when he returned. It would be published in 1847 under the title *Narrative of a Journey Round the World During the Years 1841 and 1842*. To this day it remains the best description of the areas covered by Simpson, covering ocean travel in both the northern Atlantic and Pacific oceans, canoe travel in Rupert's Land, California in the years immediately preceding Union with the United States, the Sandwich Islands (Hawaii) in its emerging nationhood, and the curiosity of Siberia and the Russian Empire. It is the world seen through the eyes of one of the most astute observers of the time, and an administrator of an empire-sized territory. All of this gave him a unique view of the world, one that deserves reading even now.

"On the morning of the 3rd of March 1841 I left London for Liverpool." So began Simpson's epic journey that was to take him overland around the world. He would travel across the widest extent of both North America and the Eurasian continent.

Simpson was not travelling alone. He had with him his new secretary, Edward Hopkins. Aboard ship out of Liverpool he recruited the ship's steward, the Gaelic-speaking John McIntyre, to serve as his manservant. Save for the train trip from London to Liverpool, McIntyre would be the only one to travel with Simpson on the entire journey around the world.

If Simpson wanted perilous adventure, he got it almost at once. Five days out of Liverpool, the captain, noting that the barometer had fallen between two and three inches during the night, concluded that a storm was approaching. Soon "it blew a perfect hurricane, during which ... the crew could barely show themselves on deck, unless sheltered from the fury of the blast." A boat and the cutwater were carried off, "much of the canvas was torn to rags, and seven of our men were severely injured." The sea "rose into mountains, whose whitened crests, shorn off as soon as formed, were scattered through the air like drifts of snow.... The sky was as dark as night; the rain fell heavily; and our ship, like a 'thing of life,' might have been supposed to struggle and groaning the agonies of dissolution." After two days of this, "the sea, still running high ... carried away her jib-boom."

But Simpson liked Boston, for there was much "to remind an Englishman of home.... Both the buildings and the inhabitants had a peculiarly English air about them. Moreover in many respects, that do not strike the eye, Boston resembles her fatherland."

From Boston the travel was by carriage and sleigh to Montreal, the roads in abominable condition, half snow, half thawed. The horses broke their traces, and galloped off, Simpson tells us, "over the hills and far away," leaving the travellers "to kick our heels in the slush." But later, the presence of "one of our [British] regiments" confirmed that they had crossed into Canada.

At Montreal, "neither meadow nor bush displayed any symptom of reviving vegetation," but on the fourth of May — two months since leaving London — the canoes ready, "the men struck up one of their hereditary ditties, and off we went amid the cheers and adieus of our assembled friends." The party was heading for Red River Settlement, 1,500 miles away.

The route was familiar to Simpson now — up the Ottawa River and into the Mattawa, then on into Lake Huron to Lake Superior. Here they found, within a month of mid-summer, that the ice was "still as firm and solid as in the depth of winter," while the thermometer stood at 73 degrees Fahrenheit.

The ice melting, the party proceeded westward, along the northern shore of Lake Superior to Fort William, then over some of the most rugged country on the continent. Only the Rainy River offered relief from toil: "from Fort Frances downwards, a stretch of nearly a hundred miles, it is not interrupted by a single impediment, while yet the current is not materially strong enough to retard an ascending traveller." Then across Lake of the Woods and down the Winnipeg River, which forms "along its rocky channels, so many falls and rapids, many of them of almost matchless grandeur."

At the great inland sea of Lake Winnipeg, they crossed the traverse to the reed-filled mouth of the Red River, and forty miles onward the travellers arrived at the middle of the continent — Red River Settlement. "Thus we had accomplished in safety our long voyage of about two thousand miles," Simpson concludes, a journey that had taken thirty-eight days from Montreal to complete.

In July, Simpson and his party set out by horse and cart for Edmonton House, eight hundred miles away.

Rupert's Land, as Simpson presents it to us, was a land of contrasts, so extreme sometimes that life and death were determined by them. The prairies in summer were of exquisite beauty, a land of "many shallow lakes … brushing the luxuriant grass with our very knees; and, on the hard ground, the surface was beautifully diversified with a variety of flowers, such as the rose, the hyacinth, and the tiger-lily…. We traversed two fields … of the rose and sweetbriar, while each loaded the air with its own particular fragrance." But in the midst of this beauty, at night the mosquitoes were "so numerous that they literally mottled the poor horses with black patches of great size, extending at the same time a very unreasonable share of their attentions to ourselves."

On the prairies, Simpson commented, "everything is in extremes — unparalleled cold and excessive heat; long droughts balanced by drenching rain and destructive hail. But it is not in climate only that these contrarieties prevail; at some seasons both whites and natives are living in wasteful abundance, on venison, buffalo, fish, and game of all kinds; while at other times they are reduced to the last degree of hunger, often passing several days without food."

Simpson's party, now consisting of nineteen persons, fifty horses, and six carts, passed over the prairies at the rate of only "four or five miles an hour, ten, twelve, or fourteen hours a day," for a progress of forty to seventy miles a day. Then again, they were into a "beautiful country, with lofty hills and long valleys, full of sylvan lakes, while the bright green of the surface, as far as the eye could reach, assumes a foreign tinge under an uninterrupted profusion of roses and blue bells."

Here were the prairies as Simpson loved them, in their infinite summer beauty, a vast inland sward covered with the rich grasses, the fields of scented flowers, the stupendous beauty, the mysterious mists, extending for 1,500 miles from Red River to the Rockies. It was a beauty that struck awe into those who saw it in those days, before the plough turned the grass and the flowers into impassive dun earth. It's little wonder that in 1857, when he addressed the Select Committee in London, Simpson did nothing to encourage agricultural settlement of the West.

Simpson and his party reached Fort Edmonton, then struck south to the Bow River, passed the site of the modern town of Banff, forced their way over the divide by a never-before-explored pass known today as Simpson Pass.

On the western side of the mountains the temperature suddenly and dramatically changed, "a change noticed by all travellers in these regions." The rill remarked upon at the summit swiftly "gathered a breadth of fifty feet." By the next day the same stream "had swollen into a hundred yards." They had reached the most dangerous part of their whole traverse of the continent:

> A very remarkable spot, known as Red Rock
> ... the ravine literally darkened by almost per-
> pendicular walls of a thousand or fifteen hun-
> dred feet in height; and, to render the chasm
> still more gloomy, the opposite crags threw
> forward each its own forest of somber pines,
> into the intervening space. The rays of the sun
> could barely find their way to the depths of
> this dreary vale, so as to render the darkness
> visible; and the hoarse murmur of the angry
> stream as it bounded to escape from the dis-
> mal jaws of its prison, only served to make
> the place more lonely and desolate. We were
> glad to emerge from this horrid gorge, which
> depressed our spirits even more than it over-
> awed our feelings.

This gorge and red rock may be viewed today at Radium Hot Springs, looking not nearly as fearsome as Simpson paints them.

Then, abruptly, they are out into "some high hills of parched clay," where "the reflection of the heat from below and the scorching sun above almost roasted us alive."

And so across an ever-varying landscape, the tired travellers moved into the Columbia Valley. Canoes carried them on to Fort Vancouver, where James Douglas reported, "Sir George, true to his pledge, arrived among us with a dashing train of Knights and squires of various dignus on the 26th of August." He had "crossed the continent of North America at its widest part, by a route of about 5,000 miles, in the space of twelve weeks of actual travelling," thus averaging 414 miles per week, or fifty-nine miles per day.

In September 1841, Simpson set out for the Russian territories with a crew of ten, "including Iroquois who spoke their own language, a Cree, a half breed of French origin, who appeared to have borrowed his dialect from both his parents; a North Briton, who understood only the Gaelic of his native hills, Canadians who of course knew French, and Sandwich Islanders [Hawaiians], who jabbered a medley of Chinook, English, &c, and their own vernacular jargon."

From Fort Nisqually (modern Tacoma, Washington), the steamer *Beaver* carried them through Puget Sound into the Strait of Georgia, past the mouth of the Fraser River, passing without notice the entrance to Burrard Inlet, the site of modern Vancouver, and into Johnstone's Strait, leading to Queen Charlotte Sound. Beyond this lay the Russian territories in North America in the Alaskan panhandle.

All along the coast Indians came to the *Beaver* "to drive a brisk trade for an hour or two," leading to handsome profits for the Company. Simpson's plan in 1828 had been to oppose the Americans ships and drive them away. Now, he is happy to report, "the absence of competition in this quarter had enabled us to put the trade on a much better footing, by the entire disuse of spirituous liquors, and by the qualified interdiction ... of the sale of arms and ammunition." So Simpson's hard work in the 1820s to recover the Columbia trade was paying off.

Then "the dangerous traverse" of open ocean lasted the whole day, and the ship entered "the smooth waters of Fitzhugh's

Sound," the channel now formed by islands to seaward and promontories on the mainland.

Farther north, Simpson found the landscape "some of the wildest scenery in nature ... thrown together in tumultuous confusion, the rivers, mere torrents ... plunge headlong in deep gulleys." Then on to Fort Stikine, where "the slime ... aided by the putridity and filth of the native villages ... oppress[ed] the atmosphere with a most nauseous perfume."

North again, glaciers plunged to the water's edge, the canals filled with ice through which the ship could scarcely force its way. The ship proceeded through thick fog and mist, and into the Russian harbour of New Archangel (Sitka), where Governor Etholine sent his compliments and welcome. They were now deep within Russian territory, but all of this landward side was under Simpson's control by agreement with the Russian American Company.

Simpson could point out with some pride that at one time the Russians and the Americans dominated the coast, yet "since 1828, however, the HBC came with energy to the coast; and now, while the Russians confine themselves to their own territory, not a single American is engaged in the branch of commerce in question."

On September 30, Simpson left New Archangel to make his retreat back to the Columbia. He was glad to leave "the dreariness of this inhospitable coast."

"Thus," said Simpson, "had I twice traversed the most extraordinary course of inland navigation in the world." A few weeks later the redoubtable Letitia Hargrave could report, "Hargrave [her husband] had a letter from the Governor dated Vancouver. He appears in great spirits and says everything is in a prosperous state. The Russians of whom they had such a dread have turned out the most delightful neighbors and in place of being rivals are excellent customers."

10

California: Nature Doing Every Thing, Man Doing Nothing

*San Francisco will to a moral certainty, sooner
or later, fall into the possession of Americans.*
— George Simpson

In early 1842, as his ship approached the California shore,
Simpson noticed an extraordinary sight, one which to his mind
summed up the totality of the California he was about to visit:

> During the whole of the twenty-ninth [January
> 1842], we lay in this state of inactivity about
> five miles from shore, which presented a level
> sward of about a mile in depth, backed by a
> high ridge of grassy slopes — the whole pas-
> tured by numerous herds of cattle and horses,
> which, without a keeper and without a fold,

were growing and fattening, whether their owners waked or slept, in the very middle of winter, and in the coldest nook of the province. Here, on the very threshold of the country, was California in a nutshell, Nature doing every thing and man doing nothing.

Nature doing everything and man doing nothing — the summation of all that he was to notice about the California that preceded union. A land so rich in plenty that labour was unnecessary, with all the evils that inactivity brings. It was to be the theme of his visit — how plenty breeds sloth and idleness corruption. As a master administrator he, unlike most who travelled in those days, was able to see the evil that bounty could bring.

At the entrance of San Francisco Bay he was reminded once more of this. The ship fell once more becalmed, its sails "flapped listlessly against the mast, the vessel heaved reluctantly on the sluggish waters; and the long swell slowly rolled the weight of the giant ocean towards the whitened strand." The lazy sails, the listless heave of the ship, the sluggish ocean, all presented a scene that "forcibly struck the imagination as an emblem of the lazy grandeur" of the land within the bay.

And so Simpson entered San Francisco Bay, lying useless in the sun, waiting for exploitation. "Time," he noted, "is a perfect glut with a community of loungers." Too lazy to fish, the inhabitants lived exclusively on beef. Where "suitable timber for ship building invites the axe at a reasonable distance," the citizens, too lazy to build, sailed on balsa rafts instead of boats. The bay, lying useless in a golden haze, turned "the very bounty of providence into a curse, corrupt[ing] a naturally indolent population by the superabundance of cattle and horses, by the readiness, in short, with which idleness can find both subsistence and recreation."

Usual amenities were unknown: No wool for coarse cloth was woven, because, "the Californians are too lazy to weave or spin — too lazy, I suspect, even to clip and wash the raw materials — that the sheep have been literally destroyed to make more room for the horned cattle.... Neither butter nor cheese, nor any preparation of milk whatsoever, is to be found in the province.... No growing of wheat, so no flour. No bread.... Meat enough to supply the fleets of England is annually either consumed by fire or left to the carrion birds."

The vast fields of cattle roamed unattended; the horsemen "did not even devote their idle hours to the tending of their herds." Villages, sunk in their lethargy, had become "sinks of profligacy and riot." Despite the efforts of the missionaries spanning decades, "very few individuals of any age can either read or write."

California, Simpson concluded, had become the "asylum and paradise of idlers, holding out to every adventurer ... the prospect of earning his bread without the sweat of his brow."

California had gained its independence from Mexico in 1836, but with freedom, Simpson observed, "the results were inevitable. Liberty degenerated into licentiousness, while power was merely another name for tyranny." The reins fell into the hands of warlords and adventurers with little interest in the public good. The results were obvious to him: "Government appears to exist only for its own sake. The grand secret of office to levy a revenue and consume it.... Every change of rulers is effected by a successful rebellion, by the triumph of force over law."

The leaders of this golden land were little better than the riff-raff that populated the villages. They had left their land defenceless, their army consisted of "superannuated troopers," while "one paltry vessel … constituted the entire line of battle of the Californian navy." Meanwhile, General Vallego, one of the more "consistent spoilers," lived fifty miles away, at Sonoma, in a vast house fifty feet in length but indifferently furnished, except for, Simpson noted, the presence of "some gaudy chairs from Woahoo [Oahu], such as the native islanders themselves often make."

Simpson could only shake his head in disbelief: "This was California all over — the richest and most influential individual in a professedly civilized settlement obliged to borrow the means of sitting from savages."

The first ladies of the province dressed in a "plain and simple gown sufficiently short to display a neatly-turned ankle, bandage their heads in a handkerchief, a swath of shawl around their shoulder, and over all, the 'beautiful and mysterious mantilla.'" Of course, the men of the upper classes — "generally tall and handsome" — are the peacocks: "round a broad-brimmed hat is tied a parti-coloured cord or handkerchief; a shirt, which is usually of the finest linen, displays on the breast a profusion of lace and embroidery; and over the shirt is thrown a cotton or silk jacket of the gayest hues, with frogs on the back, and a regiment of buttons on the breast and cuffs. [But] with such painted and gilded horsemen, anything like industry is, of course, out of the question." The men instead spent their time, "from morning to night, in billiard playing and horse racing, aggravating the evil of idleness by ruinously heavy bets.... Bear and bull baiting are the common sports … singing and dancing as common as eating and sleeping, all are musicians, everyone strumming away in turn."

As one might have expected, "the children improved on the example of their parents through the influence of a systematic education — the education which gave them the lasso as a toy in infancy, and the horse as a companion in boyhood, which in short, trained them from the cradle to be mounted bullock-hunters and nothing else."

Even the food, so abundant here, was served up without any graces. Meals, prepared in hodgepodge fashion by "native drudges, unwashed and uncombed," were served up "more than once ... in one and the same dish, beef, and tongue, and pumpkin, and garlick, and potatoes in their jackets, and cabbage, and onions, and tomato, and pepper, and Heaven knows what besides."

Before the revolution of 1836, the Catholic missions — twenty-one in number — had gathered much wealth from cattle and crops, and the cheap labour of the indigenous peoples. But with the "tendency of every revolution to make the church its first victim," the new government had "secularized the missions" by systematic plunder of their riches, confiscating the pious funds, and distributing the lands and cattle to its own followers. With intense sarcasm, Simpson points out that the plunderers set a limit to their sacrilege, leaving the "mint, anise, and cumin untouched," but carrying off "doors, and windows, and roofs, leaving the unsheltered adobes ... to the fate of Nineveh and Babylon."

This "spoliation of the missions, except as it has opened the province to general enterprise, has directly tended to nip civilization in the bud," Simpson concludes.

When California fell into Spanish hands, the missionaries moved in to "civilize" the Natives. They had been taught the

Spanish language and been put to work on the great mission estates. The appearance at least was of a productive new labour force. But the missionaries had "regarded the natives as children of life," never training them for anything more than menials on the estates. But it was all a veneer kept polished by the perseverance of the missionaries. Rather than teach them to farm, the missions had "penned the whole like cattle, and watched them like children, at the very most making them eye-servants."

With the revolutions, the "proselytes, like the cattle, were divided among the spoilers, either as menial drudges or as predial serfs." There, Simpson found "many of them too sadly broken in spirit even to marry," destined, he felt, to "soon pass away from the land of their fathers."

Though many of them were well-formed and well-grown, "every face bears the impress of poverty and wretchedness; and they are, moreover, a prey to several malignant diseases, among which … hereditary syphilis ranks as the predominant scourge alike of old and young. They are badly clothed, badly lodged, and badly fed … [on] the worst bullocks, worst joints, with bread of acorns and chestnuts. Thralls in all but the name, [they] vegetate rather than live." He felt this was all caused through the "zeal of the church."

Those Natives who had not received the missionaries' dubious hand of "civilization" were little better off. The Californians and the Natives, it turned out, "live in a state of warfare that knows no truce. The Indian makes a regular business of stealing horses, that he may ride the tame ones, and eat such as are wild.… In his turn the Californian treats the Indian, wherever he finds him, very much like a beast of prey, shooting him down, even in the absence of any specific charge, as a common pest and a public enemy." For this state of affairs, Simpson contends, "the public authorities are far more to blame than private individuals." Preoccupied as they were in extorting their salaries from the public purse, they "care[d] little for the general welfare and security" of the people. Simpson's indignation and wrath boiled to the surface at this mistreatment of these simple people:

> Let the priests treat the savage not as a child but as a man; let them consider him not as a mere machine but as a rational being; let them train him, not by physical coercion, but by motives addressed to his head and heart, to think and act for himself in the various relations of life. Above all, let them humanize the whites by the influences of religion, for, without the hearty co-operation of the colonists, the civilization of the savages can be neither complete nor permanent.

Simpson does not mince his words in summing up the future of California. This is an angry Simpson. His last word on these people may have been a gentle one:

> The Californians are a happy people, possessing the means of physical pleasure to the full, and knowing no higher kind of enjoyment.... Whatever may be the merits or demerits of Californian happiness, the good folks thrive upon it. They live long, warding off the marks of age for a period unusual even in some less trying climates. In the matter of good looks, both sexes merely give nature fair play, scouting as well the cares as the toils of life.

But laughing at the cares and the toils of life will, Simpson predicted, lead to their certain doom: "San Francisco will to a moral certainty, sooner or later, fall into the possession of Americans." English, in some sense of the word, "the richest portions of California must become."

And Simpson, of course, was right. The Californians in their torpor soon fell to Yankee energy and efficiency, the country joining the United States only eight years after Simpson's visit.

Simpson, as nowhere else in his writings, lets out his heart in his depiction of the people of California before the union. Everywhere California is the counter of Rupert's Land. In California is warmth, in Rupert's Land the killing cold; in California spoils lie for the taking in the fields, in Rupert's Land sustenance is wrung by the labour of a lifetime; the Californian leaves his lands unprotected, Rupert's Land is preserved by constant vigilance; in California justice is a mockery, in Rupert's Land the people live under laws so few the people know them perfectly.

And, of course, there is the lesson of history — California fell to the Americans, Rupert's Land remained a part of the British Empire.

11

Sandwich Islands: "By the Sweat of Their Brows"

*[They were] compelled by the necessities of nature
to earn their food by the sweat of their brows.*
— *George Simpson*

Incongruously, when Simpson first beheld the Sandwich Islands
(now the Hawaiian Islands), these jewels of the warm Pacific
appeared to him, "swelling as if a solitary iceberg in breadth
and height out of the blue ocean." It was, of course, the snowy
summit of Mauna Kea, appearing then disappearing along the
rim of the horizon from a distance of 109 miles. Then, beyond
it, the peak of Mauna Loa came into view, more distant still,
the twin sentinels marking this island chain "thrown up from
the deep by volcanic action" onto the largest ocean on Earth.
Past the great mountains they had in sight "at one and the same
time, the four Islands of Mowee [Maui], Lanai, Molokai, and

Woahoo [Oahu]." He continued: "We were, in fact, sailing along one of the eight seas [that separate the islands]." Island after island rose up, and each "grew at once in height and in breadth according to the intensity of the power that heaved it upwards from the waters."

The island of Oahu, to which their ship was heading, "bore a remarkably sterile and rugged aspect, exhibiting, at least to our comparatively distant view, nothing but desolate rocks." The island was distinguished only by the headland known as Diamond Hill — now Diamond Head. Then, rounding this cape, they saw before them "a belt of level ground, washed in front by the sea, and skirted in the rear by the continuation of the mountains."

George Simpson was at last in the harbour of Honolulu.

George tells us that travelling by sea "prepares one, by means of reading, to profit by what one may see and hear on the land." On his ocean voyage from California to Hawaii he had been reading up on these Hawaiians, and even before he landed had come to the conclusion that he was going to like these people. Here was a race in thrall to no one, who had, since Captain Cook's visit, made every attempt to control their own destinies as a people.

In 1795, King Kamehamaha the First had acquired by force of arms Maui and Oahu, while he soon after received the voluntary submissions of his royal brother of Kauai. The royal seat was set at Honolulu and later at Lahaina. A navy, originally of outriggers, had been established, now replaced by boats, which served to bring peace and protection to the harbour of Honolulu. This navy was "infinitely creditable to the Hawaiians," Simpson concluded, especially when compared to the single derelict ship that made up the Californian "navy." An army was also being raised, and while this had its humorous aspects, the contingent being small and parading with sticks for rifles, "the men as a body were strapping fellows, with the best of all uniforms, good looks, and fine figures."

Simpson could not help admiring the Hawaiians for striving for a modern government away from the misrule of local chiefs and princes, and the establishment of a political stability sufficient to secure the peace of Honolulu Harbour, where ships arrived from around the world.

These were, Simpson realized, not the shiftless lot of the Californians, basking idly in the sunshine, but a hard-working people bound by circumstances to labour for their living. "The industry of the natives," Simpson felt, "is the quality which promises to be the most conducive to their civilization. A habit, if not a love, has been implanted and cherished in them by a combination of causes more or less peculiar to their condition, which chiefly, if not wholly, resolve themselves into the niggardliness of nature and the disposition of government."

These people did not have the luxury of slaughtering cattle in the fields for their living, but were "compelled by the necessities of nature to earn their food by the sweat of their brows." There was little drunkenness, the Natives "sober even beyond the standard of clerical self-denial, drinking but little water and rarely indulging in the steaming beverage."

Unlike the Natives of the continent, Simpson found the houses here "scrupulously clean and neat, presenting, in this aspect, a wonderful contrast to the filth and confusion of most of the native lodges of the continent."

He found that the Natives themselves were a garrulous, happy people, who "must speak or die, and never meet ... without indulging ... in a perpetual din of gossip and banter ... the women jabbering and joking in their inarticulate jargon." Even work was turned into play, he said: statutory labour was "the most entertaining part of the business, the work gangs of forty accompanied by its full compliment of shouting and giggling women; and one whole gang might be seen running and laughing with a log of wood on their shoulders, which four or five men might have conveyed with ease, evidently succeeding to their own perfect satisfaction in converting the toil into pleasure."

Here was a people after Simpson's own heart, and he was determined to help them secure their independent place in the world.

In California, Simpson had foreseen the ultimate end of the idle Californians in a takeover by Americans, and had no pity for them. But for the islanders he saw, even as the Natives were struggling to create an independent nation for themselves, that "the teachers of a better faith were wending their way towards the Sandwich Islands.

"In this archipelago," he reflected, "civilization is sweeping the aborigines from the land of their fathers ... without placing in their stead better than themselves."

But this petty "belligerent spirit" aside, Simpson had, in fact, arrived in the islands at a critical time in their history. For several years the government had received threats from the French squadron in the Pacific. The British consul, Captain Robert Charlton, was stirring up trouble over some land claims. And the American missionaries on the islands seemed to be pushing them toward an American takeover. It was widely expected on the islands that one or the other of these countries would soon declare sovereignty over them.

Simpson quickly took the measure of the situation and sided with the Hawaiians for their independence. He listened to what had been done, then expressed his opinion that these measures would not succeed. He recommended that a commission be sent from the islands on this great business, with authority to negotiate treaties with Great Britain, France, and the United States.

Simpson took for his assistant the Reverend William Richards, the government's translator and recorder, who introduced him to the Reverend Mr. Baldwin, "who complained loudly of the overbearing conduct of the British and French consuls, adding that letters on the subject had been written to Queen Victoria but had not been answered; and at his request I undertook to become the bearer of further dispatches."

Thus began a series of secret meetings between Simpson and Richards with the premier. It all seemed so cloak and dagger, and Simpson must have enjoyed the mystery of it: "At night I again visited the premier by special appointment, accompanied by Mr. Richards. We entered the Fort after dark by the postern gate, where the sentries, evidently expecting us, permitted us to pass without challenge; and we were then conducted into the House by a fellow resembling, in office and demeanour, the mutes of an oriental harem."

Interviews were held "at nightfall," or "after dark," while "Mr. Charlton, partly from curiosity, and partly from a suspicion of treason, was rendered quite restless and unhappy by being excluded from our confidence." At last "the papers were submitted to the king and premier, who then decided, agreeably to a suggestion of mine, Mr. Richards should proceed to England as envoy, being for this purpose associated with the governor and deputy-governor of the HBC and myself, and that we should have authority to make arrangements on behalf of the Hawaiian government, not merely with England, but also with France and the United States."

By previous arrangement, a young Hawaiian of "gentlemanly bearing," Timothy Haalilio, would accompany Richards. All this was done within the scope of Simpson's six weeks on the islands.

Meanwhile, with Simpson continuing his journey and Richards and Haalilio gone on their mission to Washington and England, mischief was afoot in the islands, instigated almost entirely by the machinations of George's cousin Alexander Simpson. He joined with the British consul, Captain Richard Charlton, to annex the islands to the British Empire. According to Ralph Kuykendall, historian of the islands, Alexander was "a man of ability, a lover of intrigues, and in the Hawaiian situation of 1842 found a field admirably adapted to his talents and political hopes."

The same writer could not help commenting that "one can scarcely avoid feeling that they [Alexander and Charlton] deliberately sought to create a situation which would make British intervention inevitable ... [by which] the claims of British subjects would be made the excuse for adding the Islands to the British Empire."

With Alexander and Charlton not sure what Simpson was up to, it was decided that Charlton travel to London to deliver complaints to the foreign office in person. Alexander was appointed as acting British consul to the islands, an appointment not accepted by the Hawaiian government. Meanwhile, Rear Admiral Richard Thomas, commander of the British squadron in the Pacific, received a letter from Alexander outlining the problems as Alexander painted them. Thomas sent Captain Lord George Paulet of the British frigate *Carysfort* with a vague instruction to "watch over and protect British subjects."

When the *Carysfort* arrived in Honolulu, Alexander "immediately went on board and told his prejudiced story." Paulet was brought completely around to Alexander's views. Under

Alexander's clever ploys, demands were made to the Hawaiian government, and ultimatums given under threats to bombard the city. Fearing he could do nothing, the king capitulated, the British flag was raised, and for five months the islands were under British rule. All of this was done, of course, without the authority of the British government in London, and even as Sir George Simpson was persuading the foreign office to respect the islands' independence.

When George Simpson returned to London from his world journey, he set up a meeting with the British Foreign Secretary, the Earl of Aberdeen. He managed to sway the skeptical minister, and "transformed the British position to one of complete acceptance of his views." Simpson then accompanied Haalilio and Richards to Brussels and Paris, and won Belgian and French acceptance for independence for the Sandwich Islands. Britain formally recognized the independence of the islands, and an Anglo-French convention was signed in March 1843, pledging respect for the territorial integrity and independence of the islands. This was a complete vindication and victory for Sir George Simpson.

The British government moved quickly to restore Hawaiian independence. Charlton was recalled as consul to the islands, Lord Paulet was told to go back to sea and mind his own business, and Alexander Simpson, stripped of his acting-consulship, "fulminated in the newspapers and relieved his feelings by publishing a book in which his views were expressed with much candor." Then he went home to Scotland in a snit, and used his brother Thomas to attack his celebrated cousin. If Sir George Simpson's reputation has been tarnished in the eyes of the world today, it is due in large part to the scurrilous if clever attack on him by his vengeful cousin.

All of this activity on behalf of the Sandwich Islands was just an aside for Simpson, amid the course of his work for the HBC and his journey round the world, but it illustrates the remarkable ability of the man to sway events when he put his mind to it.

12

Siberia:
"They Looked as If Actually Afloat"

*The whole population of every village, whether
by day or by night, flocked to see us.*
— *George Simpson*

Perhaps Jules Verne got the idea for his novel *Around the World
in Eighty Days* from reading Simpson's *Narrative of a Journey
Round the World*. If so, the kernel of the plot came from his
Siberian exploits, as he rushed helter-skelter among some of the
strangest characters in his experience.

As Simpson approached the shores of Siberia, the town of Okhotsk
appeared to be floating on the water. This was no mirage of shining palaces: "a more dreary scene can scarcely be imagined." The
town was "standing on a shingly head so low and flat as not to be

distinguished ... from the adjacent waters. We saw nothing but a number of wretched buildings, which seemed to be in the sea ... while from their irregularity they looked as if actually afloat."

Like the Russian witch Baba Yaga doing her crazy dance upon the waters, much of the Siberian trip would involve similarly skewed images. The centre of the town was a stagnant marsh, "which must be the nursery of all sorts of malaria and pestilence." And all around, "not a tree, and hardly even a green blade, is to be seen within miles of the town." Summer was three months long, "succeeded by nine months of dreary winter," when scurvy raged through the town.

Welcome to Siberia.

On June 27, Simpson set off for the town of Yakutsk on the banks of the Lena, eight hundred miles away, his "little band consisting of two fellow travellers and myself, and my servant," the whole under the protection of a Cossack outrider, the horses under the direction of a Yakuti named Jacob, whose face reminded Simpson of a monkey in the London zoo, who needed the crack of the Cossack's whip to hurry him along.

Hardly had they left the town when they "met an apparently interminable line of about six hundred horses carrying goods" to the settlement. This was the first of many, for Simpson found that the "road was absolutely alive with caravans and travellers, each consisting of four or five hundred horses ... all proceeding to Okhotsk with goods, provisions and cattle." With so many horses in use, "the unfortunate brutes here lie down to die, in great numbers, through famine and fatigue, and this road was more thickly strewed with their bones than any part of the Saskatchewan with those of the buffalo."

On July 10 the temperature was extreme, the air being 80 degrees in the shade, while snow still covered the hilltops. The height of land was reached, with the rivers flowing to the Pacific or the Arctic, and "large fields of perpetual snow and ice." At one point the land was covered with stunted timber, glaciers everywhere, and then the scenery changed, "being generally well-wooded and often romantic." Halfway to Yakutsk, "the scenery began to lose its alpine character, the mountains flattening down to hills." Then, from another mountaintop, the party "obtained a beautiful view of the mountains ... their uniformly conical shape [presented] the appearance of so many gigantic molehills."

At last, after a trip lasting seventeen days, across more than eight hundred miles of forests and mountains, the Lena River and the town of Yakutsk were reached, the town created to harvest mastodon tusks buried in river mud twelve thousand years before, thrown up again by the frosts. The Lena, "one of the grandest rivers in the world," was here five or six miles wide and took the party two and a half hours to cross. The town of Yakutsk, with its spires and cupolas, was stretched along the banks, two thousand versts from its source, about 1,300 versts from its outlet into the Arctic seas, and only 450 versts from the Arctic Circle. (A verst was an old Russian measurement of distance nearly equal to a modern kilometre.)

Though thousands of miles from civilization, Simpson found the town split into quarrelling factions. "Their duties may be a toil," he comments, "but their animosities are evidently a pleasure." On the other hand, the simple Russian pleasure of drinking to excess was enjoyed by all. At the banquet to greet his arrival, the "viands were numerous and excellent, consisting of soups, fish, beef, veal, fowls wild and tamed, with pastry, sweets, and ices ... the whole accompanied by wines in abundance." The dances that followed "being kept up with great spirits, in all its form of waltzing, quadrilling, gallopading, &c, till two in the morning."

"Next day," Simpson comments, "as any reasonable reader might expect, I dined at home." But he himself was to host one of the most peculiar entertainments among the Yakuti — the feast of the gluttons. Two Yakuti were selected for the contest. "I had a dinner prepared for them of two poods of beef, boiled [70 pounds], and one pood [35 pounds] of butter melted ... for each of the two, while the liquor was in common." They ate till "their eyes were starting from their heads, wallowing prostrate on the earth, their stomachs projecting into a brace of kettledrums, the butter, apparently in its purity, making an outlet at every pore.... After such surfeits, the victors remain, for three or four days, in a state of stupor, neither eating nor drinking; and meantime they are rolled about ... with a view to the promoting of digestion — an operation which the slipperiness of their surfaces renders particularly difficult." Simpson adds, "Two of these gormandizers, one for the bride and another for the bridegroom, form part of the entertainment at every native wedding."

But such gluttony was not confined to the Yakuti alone, as Simpson brings to the reader's attention the enormous medical officer — "a fat, unwieldy apoplectic man" —who sat at table, "never opening his mouth except for the discharge of the one special duty that was before him." On his tours of inspection, the man needed "an assortment of the mechanical powers," being "hoisted up a steep hill by means of ropes and pulleys, the horses having refused to move him on any terms."

The Lena River was wide and sluggish with a slow current, the channel separated often with islands and sandbars. From Yakutsk

to Irkutsk the river was some two thousand versts long. Travel
was by scows, lined and tracked all the way, with horses changed
regularly so that movement could continue for the full twenty-
four hours of each day. Accommodation was so cramped, they
were "huddled together, nearly four days and nights, without
space to stretch our legs or even to enjoy the full swing of a com-
fortable yawn."

At last, the headwaters of the Lena reached, the party took
to carriages "unrivalled in point of whirling, and jolting, and
thumping," the whole contingent travelling "on a formidable line
of eight carriages." They were now crossing the Bratsky Steppe,
a "magnificent prairie … studded with Barat settlements, while
throughout, cattle, horses, goats, and sheep were grazing on the
rich pastures all round," reminding Simpson of "the boundless
prairies of the Assiniboine."

Arriving at last at Irkutsk, which stands on the shores of
Lake Baikal, Simpson remarked that he was "the first traveller
in the world to stand on the shores of the two greatest bodies
of fresh waters in the world." The other body of water, of course,
was Lake Superior.

On August 15, 1842, Simpson left Irkutsk, the party having
"the Emperor's commands to facilitate my movements in every
possible way." Travel was by *tarantasse*, a coach "made so that
sleep in bed is possible while the coach can travel twenty-four
hours a day," as St. Petersburg was still a great distance away,
and an early Siberian winter about to set in. The entourage left
in torrents of rain, and "to be jostled through 4,000 miles of
quagmire was by no means a pleasant anticipation." Simpson
was now crossing the great Siberian plain, an area settled by
convicts. As was to be expected, despite vigilance, several items
were stolen from their carriage.

Holidays in Siberia, he found, were "celebrated by drunkenness." A church being consecrated in Krasnoyarsk resulted in the town being overrun "for most of the night with drunken males and females." At another stop, the postmaster was "drunk and stupid." The farther they advanced to the westward "the more rapidly the roads, the posthouses, and the horses degenerate." Everywhere, he said, he found "negative churlishness." They passed a church that had been burnt on Easter Sunday, and many would have perished, but for the fact that "the inhabitants, according to time-hallowed tradition, were [at home] hopelessly drunk."

Simpson declared Yennisei the worst-governed district in all Siberia. Gold had been found in the rivers, and the populace had abandoned farming for the washeries. Women's charms were "estimated by the weight, not of herself, but of her gold. A pood is a very good girl … two or three poods are clearly twice or thrice as good as a wife." And in winter, when the washeries were frozen, the gold diggers spend "a winter of idleness, vagabondism, and dissipation." In all, the washeries "have too often become dens of drunkenness and riot," so that various governors have had to visit the fields to curb the turbulent and profligate conduct of the adventurers.

Nothing improved. At Tomsk "the road was execrable, and the night dismal and wet.… Everything seems to become worse, the roads abominable, the stages long, the country dreary, the stations comfortless, the delays constant, the postmasters uncivil." At the Kid River, a tributary of the Ob, Simpson and his party "spent three hours in crossing." He admitted that "cold, wet, sleepy, and unwell as I was, I thought this the most miserable portion of my whole journey."

Now the travel and the weather caught up with Simpson. There was "nothing to eat but black bread and sour milk, and most vexatious delays at every station." As the result of "a severe cold caught at the crossing of the Kid River, I went to bed in no very good humour, though this was the first time in fourteen days that I had doffed my clothes and slept out of the carriage." But even that night was hardly a luxury, as the landlady in the next room "kept sending forth, during the whole night, coughs, sneezes, and sighs, with various other noisy tokens of her whereabouts."

But at last the weather did improve. At a town on Sunday noon, "the good people were just coming out of church, while their less scrupulous brethren and sisters of the adjacent villages were celebrating the day as usual, by getting drunk — or rather, by continuing drunk."

Now, something strange was happening: "The whole population of every village, whether by day or by night, flocked to see us — the males all uncovered, and the females incessantly bowing. The secret gradually leaked out that our friends ahead [their Cossack guards], as much perhaps for their own convenience as our glory, had insinuated that I was an ambassador from the Emperor of China to the Czar, while the simple peasants, according to the natural growth of all marvellous stories, had of their own accord pronounced me to be the Brother of the Sea and Moon himself." Accordingly, royal treatment was afforded at all stations, and "we were decidedly the greatest men who had ever been seen to the east of the Uralian Mountains.... As the roads were excellent, we enjoyed the joke, whirling along at twelve or fifteen versts an hour."

In three nights and two days the party travelled from Omsk to Tobolsk, which Simpson found full of interest. Women, for instance, who are spinsters on their mother's death, were sold to the highest bidder by the nearest relative for his personal emolument. Simpson wrote: "the damsels don't seem to dislike the practice." An old man, knowing that England was in the west, "could not conceive how we, being English, could be coming from the east … assuring me that they had no other way to come." He visited a military school that trained boys as interpreters, preparatory to the subjection of the Kirghiz. He witnessed army discipline Russian style, the hospitals full of "patients suffering from military punishment, all actually delirious."

Throughout the journey, they had been passing parties of convicts sent into exile in Siberia. As they approach European Russia, the roads become crowded. In eastern Siberia, the groups consisted of "seventy or eighty fellows chained together in sixes or so, by light handcuffs, and escorted by ten or twelve Cossacks." With nearly sixteen thousand convicts arriving in Siberia each year, it's little wonder that Simpson found the country more settled than he had thought.

At Tiumen he was referred to as "General Simpson, a great man." Simpson described the village of Kamishloff as miserable, but after finding that a previous traveller had called it pretty, concluded: "So on the united authorities of my predecessor and myself … Kamishloff is a 'pretty miserable' place."

At last the barrier between Asia and Europe was reached — the Ural Mountains separating European Russia from Asiatic Siberia — but strangely, Simpson notices that "the ascent and descent of the mountains were so gentle, that we were barely conscious of climbing a ridge that divided two continents."

On into European Russia they sped, now finding the roads swarming with "footpads, who were said to be infesting the road in considerable numbers." They arrived in Kazan, only to find that it had been recently burned to the ground, with "rows of gutted houses, as cold and dead as if they had been unchanged for a century." European Russia was hardly an improvement: "The travelling here was worse by many degrees than in Siberia.

The horses were bad, the road heavy, and the delays apparently just what the postmaster chose to make them." Speed could be maintained only by bribing the postmaster, and "a few roubles, whenever I yielded to the imposition, never failed to accelerate movements."

While the Russian peasants seemed a happy and contented lot, their appearance did not impress Simpson: "Neither males nor females can, in my opinion, boast much of their beauty. The women are generally red-faced, red-handed, red-heeled, strong-featured wenches of substantial build, while the men, as their prerogative, surpass them in all these masculine accomplishments."

Moscow was reached, at last — a sorry city in the mid-nineteenth century. It had been abandoned as a capital more than a century before, and burnt down during the French occupation in 1812. Now, far from finding hoped-for elegance, Simpson found the city a "perfect eyesore of rectangular beds of cabbage in all the tribes, carrots, turnips, onions, and such like." So the party did not tarry to enjoy the magnificence of the Kremlin, but hurried on to St. Petersburg. For the first time in their long journey, the road from Moscow to St. Petersburg presented the luxury of "700 versts of macadamized road."

At last the spires of the city founded by Peter the Great appeared on the horizon, and at "about eight in the morning on the 8th of our English October, we drove into St. Petersburg, thus terminating our travels through the Russian Empire about five-and-twenty weeks after our arrival at Sitka.... The distance from Ochotsk to St. Petersburg, included stoppages, had occupied ninety-one days, during which time we had traversed about seven thousand miles." He had, Simpson could say with satisfaction, "seen more of this colossal empire than any foreigner, living or dead."

As Simpson left the Russian Empire, he could not restrain himself from singing the praises of the Russian Emperor, Nicholas I, and by so doing, reminding his readers of his own position in the world:

> Nicholas ... is the autocrat of three continents, the master of the most extensive dominions of ancient and modern times, as an object, not merely of philanthropic interest, but of mysterious awe.

A gentle reminder of what had been said of Simpson himself, who ruled with supreme authority as the head of the most extended dominions in the known world — the Emperor of Russia, and Queen of England, and the President of the United States excepted.

From St. Petersburg, Simpson travelled to Hamburg, and "in five days more I reached London, having ... accomplished my journey round the world ... the whole being completed within the space of nineteen months and twenty six days."

Although Simpson had been ill during much of the last stages of his journey, and spent his week in St. Petersburg in bed "in consequence of a most severe and obstinate cold," Letitia Hargrave could report that "The Gov'r got home too & was well all but his eyes, old Mrs. Simpson says, in great health & spirits & not like a man who had undergone privation or made a tour of the world."

13

Glow of Power: Riding with the Emperor

He had the rare qualities of true leadership. He could win men's allegiance with a smile, or compel it with an iron will.
— *George Bryce*

By the 1850s, Sir George Simpson's method of canoe travel had been honed to a high degree of perfection, designed in its majesty to strike awe into the beholder, to impress the Natives, the paddlers, the clerks, and the chief factors, and to gain their respect and friendship. The governor's progress through his domain was a phenomenon that was remarked upon when it happened, and recalled with the deepest nostalgia long after its splendour had passed into history.

Amongst those who recalled Simpson's passage through the country were Archibald McDonald, who accompanied Simpson in 1828; Frances Simpson (1830); Sir Frederich Graham, a sporting gentleman (1847); and new recruit Henry Moberly, who joined him in 1854.

Image A-02878 courtesy of Royal BC Museum, BC Archives.

Simpson's image as it appeared in his Narrative of a Journey Round the World, *1847.*

Simpson learned quickly the power of pomp and ceremony, not for itself, but for its effect. "The more form that is observed, the greater weight it will have," he wrote. In the spring of 1821, as he was about to leave the Athabasca in triumph, he wished to have that achievement impressed upon the world. He ordered a "racer" canoe to facilitate the speed that would later become his trademark, and rushed through the rivers and past the posts, the first to broadcast his successes in the North. His next canoe was exquisitely crafted. He called it *Eclipse* — and proceeded to eclipse all speed records in the land. It was a pace and a tradition he carried out to the last days of his life.

When Simpson travelled, say, from Lachine to Norway House for the Council of the Northern Department, he did so in a beautifully made birchbark canoe. Those who saw it were inspired by its craftsmanship. His young bride, Frances, described it as "airy and elegant beyond description." McDonald described it with a sense of awe:

> The Governor's [canoe] was the most beautiful thing of the kind I ever saw; beautiful in its lines of faultless fineness, and in its form and every feature; the bow, a magnificent curve of bark gaudily but tastefully painted, and would have made a Roman rostrum of old hang its diminished head. The paddles were painted red with vermilion, were made to match, and the whole thing in its kind was of faultless grace and beauty — beauty in the sense of graceful and perfect fitness to its end.

With this canoe, the legend of George Simpson was born.

It is spring in Quebec. In Lachine all is bustle, all — engagés and bourgeois alike — are astir in the anticipation of the start of the shipping season:

> The interest with which the trip is looked forward to and the pleasure with which its end is welcomed, are apparently antagonistic statements, but both are real among the voyageurs. The change of scene and employment experienced in travelling outweighs the inconvenience the memory of which enables men to appreciate a settled home on their return.

Just before the ice went out on Lake St. Louis, the canoemen — French Canadians, Natives, and Mètis — would begin their traditional celebrations. Weary of the long, uneventful winter, and all agog at the thought of getting out on the rivers and trails again, they would gather at Lachine two weeks in advance and spend their days and nights "dancing to the fiddle and the concertina, singing the chansons of old France, making love to their womanfolk (or each other's), and spinning those fantastic yarns of theirs which gave rise to the saying, '*Les voyageurs n'ont jamais vu les petits loups!*'" ["Voyageurs never saw small wolves."]

As might be expected, the flowing bowl was the pivot around which these festivities resolved and, as the time of bidding farewell to the wives and sweethearts drew near, there were few who did not make full use of it, either to increase their joys or to drown their sorrows, as the case might be. It was, therefore, the aim of the Company officers in charge to keep the time of embarkation a secret, giving the men plenty to do and then suddenly leaving on very short notice. By this means, a final grand carousal was often prevented, and the men set off on the long voyage in a more or less sober state.

The cargoes loaded, the new recruits seated, the brigade would set off up the Ottawa River for posts across the continent.

Then it was the turn of Governor Simpson to prepare for his annual journey to the Northern Council. The pomp and ceremony of his departure far surpassed the ragged departure of the brigades that had preceded him. Simpson travelled in splendour, accompanied on the first day by several canoes filled with Company dignitaries. A chance passerby at Lachine was witness to one such departure:

> Sir George Simpson was just starting for the seat of his government via the Ottawa River. With him were some half-dozen officers, civil and military, and the party was escorted by six or eight Nor'West canoes — each thirty or forty feet long, manned by some twenty-four indians, in the full glory of war paint, feathers, and most dazzling costumes. To see these stately boats, with their no less stately crews, gliding with measured stroke, in gallant procession, on their way to the vasty wilderness of the Hudson's Bay Company territory, with the British flag displayed at each prow, was a sight never to be forgotten.

For travel through the wilds, the brigade did not suffer privations. Simpson's party consisted of two, sometimes three, canoes. The lead canoe held Simpson and his personal entourage; the second canoe held others travelling to the territories

— sometimes new officers and their families, or the aristocracy of England going out for the excitement of the buffalo shoot. For them, canoe travel was a veritable luxury. Said Graham,

> I can recommend this mode of traveling to the lazy man. One lies down on blankets or skins or whatever couch has been prepared; the motion of the canoe after the first day is positively delightful, and the judicious traveler takes care to lay in a stock of books and cigars to occupy the day. Nothing to be done there but read and smoke: for one soon tires of the stories which the half-breeds tell and of the plaintive French songs which they chant in time to the paddles.

Simpson's canoe held two waterproof trunks (for his clothes), an egg basket, a basket holding the day's meals, a travelling case holding six wine bottles, cups and saucers, a teapot, sugar basin, spoons, cruets, glasses and tumblers, fishing gear, tea, sugar, and salt — he also mentions a bag of biscuits, a bale of hams, and a keg of butter.

In the lead canoe sat Governor Simpson, his manservant, and his secretary to whom he dictated letters. When the pace seemed too slow, Moberly recalled, Simpson "raised his arm and slipped his fingers in the water. The steersman no sooner noticed this than he put added force into his stroke, the others followed suit, and the canoe fairly leaped ahead."

In the 1830s the boats were manned by "strong, active, fine-looking Canadians," but by the 1850s Simpson used a "picked crew of Iroquois canoemen from Caughnawaga, above

Montreal ... there are no better in the world," Moberly wrote. In Simpson's express canoe, when leaving a station or arriving at one, these boatmen "were dressed in sky blue capots, scarlet sashes, high scarlet night caps, and moccasins." But once away from the stations, they wore old clothes and sang little. They paddled silently and steadily, their breath needed for the sixty oar strokes per minute that Simpson required. On portages, their pretty costumes put aside, and dressed in nothing but their loincloths, these men to Graham presented a ghastly picture:

> Men terribly exhausted. The Iroquois carrying the canoes looking like fiends, their shirts off, their skin like heated copper, and their long black hair all loose, with their wild black eyes glowing like hot coals. Each man jumped into the river as soon as the canoes were by, and a flounder or two, to cool themselves, took the back track for another load, just as fresh as at starting.

After a particularly gruelling portage, Simpson would hand round a beaker of rum to praise the job well done. If Natives were helping on the portage, the filet was not handed out. But the voyageurs were not cheated. McDonald later recalled that the brigade stopped early in the evening so the men could enjoy "two or three extra glasses of spirits ... which they would have had in making the portage had no Indians been about."

The voyageurs were fed a steady diet of pemmican — a mixture of pounded dried buffalo meat and fat — energy-rich to keep up the pace eighteen hours a day. However, when the brigade was lucky enough to kill a moose near the shore, Simpson indulged the whole party with a "half holyday" from afternoon until the following morning, in a continued succession of "eating, roasting, and boiling."

When travelling, Simpson was in his element as nowhere else in his life. On his earlier voyages, no mere passenger, Simpson himself became the brigade commander. At an encampment, at two in the morning, it was Simpson marching through the sleepers to rouse the tired men. At seven to the minute they put ashore for breakfast. Thirty minutes were allotted to this task, then Simpson would shout, "Take away!" and the meal was ended, eaten or not, and the trip continued.

The local Natives were not neglected. When a brigade stopped at a post where they were present, "the Indians placed themselves in rows, on either side of the path leading to the house, and smiled, and appeared much pleased when spoken to." Simpson would gather the chiefs to him, introduce any new factor or trader to them, and then he "addressed them at some length, congratulated them on their good behaviour, counselled them against the use of spirituous liquors, and advised them to conserve the beaver." Then, "as a matter of great indulgence," each was given a glass of weak rum and a quantity of tobacco. When Frances Simpson saw these chiefs in 1830, she described them as "decked in all their finery ... and smiles ... [they] seemed much pleased ... when spoken to." But often they were as Graham observed them — "the Chief an ill-looking rascal, with a long coat and leggings of bright scarlet, attended by a suite of tag-rag and bobtail in all colours of the rainbow."

Simpson was an excellent judge, McDonald recalled. On the 1828 trip he had to give a verdict on a case

of assault by one man on another, under suspicion of tampering with his wife. The verdict — for

> His Excellency seems also to have been chosen
> as Jury — was "not proven," with a recommen-
> dation to the accused not to try that sort of thing
> again and by way of "earnest" a small penalty was
> imposed … which money was at once tendered,
> but was indignantly rejected, whereupon … it
> was made over … to buy liquor at the fort…. The
> beauty of the judgement … was that it pleased
> not either party, and not a little frightened both
> out of their impropriety.

So everyone won, even the bystanders, who not only rel-
ished the verdict but the tipple, as well.

Simpson's speed of travel depended on a close eye on the
watch. When a council of chief traders was held, as at Fort
William in 1854, Simpson spelled out the time to the exact
minute. On this occasion, young Moberly observed:

> As Sir George stepped ashore he turned to the
> head Indian guide and announced, "at ten min-
> utes past six o'clock we start," adding to the chief
> factor in charge, "Council meets at one o'clock.
> Just two and a half hours for feasting and talking;
> then to business.".… At five o'clock the council
> rose. General conversation followed until five
> minutes after six, when Sir George shouted, "All
> Aboard!".… Each man took his place, and at
> exactly ten minutes past six, we pushed out.

There was good reason to resume the trip at six in the evening.
By this manoeuvre, Moberly said, the crews were deprived of any

opportunity "for debauchery or whisky-buying, a strict watch was necessary until they could be isolated in camp on a small island in the lake." In 1820, Simpson had been delayed for days while the boat crews debauched at Norway House on bootlegged whisky. This was Simpson's answer to ensure such a delay did not occur again. But while the men were protected from the debauch en route, the canoes held a keg of liquor (called the Dutchman) from which the people were "drammed" four times a day. This, the voyageurs called the "filet," or "trickle." In this way the men were kept in a pleasant alcoholic haze, which bolstered their spirits, encouraged their songs, and spurred them to greater effort.

In the early days, desertion was a problem with the young recruits going to the Northwest for the first time. Suddenly confronted with the relentless pace of a Simpson canoe, they wanted no part of it. Some fled to the forests, only to be hunted down, sometime four or five hours being given over to the task. When found, the deserters were summarily court martialled by the old voyageurs and given ten lashes of the leather strap. Later, on the portages, Graham noted, "The poor *mangeurs de lard* [new recruits] terribly cooked! Loads were left, and thrashings administered by the old hands, in some cases, to make them carry through. Cruel work!"

The traverse of the north shore of Lake Superior posed the dangers of the elements: it was risky business travelling in heavily laden canoes on an open, rolling sea. In 1847, Graham's craft was nearly swamped:

> Blowing very hard from the N.E., and the sea rising fast, the coast all rocks and precipice. It came on at last to blow fearfully with heavy squalls. The sail was made fast as usual. We took in four

reefs, and reduced the sail to one half, the sea
increasing every minute, so that we were in danger when ever we had to cross from the lee of one
island to another. At last the storm rose to such a
height that we were glad to run into the first bay
we could find. Our canoe was nearly swamped
in running the narrows leading thereto by the
heavy following seas, wherein we might all have
met a watery grave. We camped in the rain, in a
snug nook among the rocks. A jolly supper in
our tents; then a chat around the fire, and to bed.

On such occasions, Simpson had his passengers join him
in his tent, where they were treated to "eggs and milk ... rice
pudding and cream, and two glasses of wine."

For sporting gentleman Graham, when the weather was fine,
"the motion was perfectly easy, and it is the most delightful mode
of travelling that can be imagined. It was a very bonnie journey
among thousands of wooded islands, through the channels of
which we twisted about throughout the day." The final long traverse to Fort William was made in the dark, the men fortified
with the filet, and in this way they "crossed over very merrily, the
crews of the three canoes (thanks to the filet) being very musically
inclined, and singing 'Belle Rose' and 'La Noisette' in chorus the
whole way."

Fighting was a common occurrence among the voyageurs,
and George himself would step in to end the furor. Frances
recalled one such episode in 1830:

Mr. Simpson was asleep at the time, but the
noise woke him, and put him in nearly as

great a passion as the combatants, upon whom
he bestowed a shower of blows with a paddle
which lay at hand, and that brought an immediate cessation of hostilities.

It was Simpson's habit to take a swim in the morning, to get rid of
woodlice and ticks, no matter what the state of the weather. Henry
Moberly, the young recruit, who felt he should join the governor
in this "extremely reprehensible habit," reported such an occasion,
when the air was icy cold and snowflakes wafted down:

> Every morning at that hour it was his practice
> to strip and take a plunge in the cold water,
> and being [loath] to be beaten by an old man,
> I had kept him company. This morning proved
> no exception to the rule, and I could not help
> feeling that I was a martyr to my chief's perni-
> cious custom, though I was bound to admit it
> was a wholesome enough one.

On the trail, Simpson used the opportunity to assist newly
appointed clerks to get to know the system and the men who
worked in it. Although Moberly presents it as an isolated joke,
George probably played this prank on every new officer recruit
who travelled with him:

> Sir George, who loved a quiet joke, played a
> good one at the expense of the officers and my

unworthy self.... He introduced me as the new chief factor of Saskatchewan.... I was seated among the "big bugs" and to carry off the joke Sir George took wine with me before anyone else. That settled it, though I myself thought it was merely an act of courtesy. This joke he carried through at all the posts we touched until we reached Norway House at the North end of Lake Winnipeg. Incidentally, I benefited from it considerably, for it gave me opportunities for becoming friendly with a number of the commissioned officers whose acquaintance, owing to the strict discipline observed, it might otherwise have taken me some years to make.

This incident stayed with young Moberly for the rest of his life, and in his extreme old age (he lived to be 96), he recalled the joke as a memorable one in his life. Simpson's purpose was not just the practical joke, not just a way of introducing a young clerk to the system, but also a way to gain the life-long respect of the clerk for the "Great Company." Moberly related another practical joke, probably also played on all young recruits:

We remained at Fort Alexander for dinner, and here I was made a victim of another joke. The Governor passed me a dish which I promptly declined. He urged me to try it but I still refused. At last he asked me why I did not touch it. "Sir George," I replied, "I may be a green man, but you won't catch me eating bear's drippings." This brought a roar of laughter from all sides.

> The Governor then ate a portion of the deli-
> cacy himself, upon which I made bold to test it
> and to my surprise found it extremely good. It
> proved to be berry pemmican of the best qual-
> ity, made of dried pounded buffalo tongues,
> marrowfat, sugar, and dried Saskatoon berries.
> In appearance it was exactly what I had called it.

The arrival of the brigade at a major post, such as Norway House, was an occasion for great pomp and ceremony. A messenger was sent ahead to let the factor know that the governor would soon be arriving. A few miles from the post, Simpson stopped the brigade, and put ashore. Here the boatmen washed and shaved, and put on their best clothes, the red shirts and trousers and L'Assomption belts, and a new feather in their caps. Simpson himself wore his best business suit and top hat. Then the brigade proceeded in full regalia to the post. When the governor's canoes were seen approaching, the chief factor fired the post's cannons, rifles were fired into the air, and the hurrahs of everyone in camp added to the din. In the canoes, Simpson's men answered by firing their own rifles into the air, while the boatmen's rowing songs rang across the water. On landing, Simpson stepped ashore, or was carried ashore, and formal greetings were taken by the governor and the factor.

After Lake Superior, the longest traverse was of Lake Winnipeg. For Moberly, the travelling was done with expedition:

> A fine steady breeze was blowing when we
> arrived at Lake Winnipeg, so we up sail and
> with both canvas and paddlers drove to the
> end of the lake without once putting ashore.

At meal time the two canoes were brought together, the outside men paddled while the others ate; they then changed positions, and when all were finished we carried on as before.

The voyageurs, who had toiled so mightily to transport the governor, always looked forward to the end of the journey, for then the reward was theirs, when the boatmen were treated to the regale. One such celebration was recalled by Frances Simpson:

On stopping to prepare for dinner, Mr. Simpson gave all the Wine & Liquor that remained to the men, who made it into Punch in their large cooking Kettle, and regaled thereon, till some of them were "powerfully refreshed." This debauch ... infused into our crew a degree of artificial strength & spirits, otherwise we should not have reached Fort Garry, as they were quite overpowered with sleep and fatigue, but after it began to operate, they paddled and sung, with much gaiety.

The governor's arrival at Norway House was celebrated with a sumptuous banquet shared by the governor, the factors, and all of his traders, clerks, and interpreters, all seated according to their rank. The governor himself had brought fine wines and European delicacies not otherwise seen in the Indian territories. Young Moberly, who still held the title of "Chief Factor of Saskatchewan," was given the seat of honour on one side of the governor with the chief factor on the other. Simpson first drank wine with his young recruit, and then a meal of extravagant proportions was indulged in:

> [It was] rather a banquet, one such as, I think,
> could scarcely be provided today at any price;
> smoked and salted buffalo tongues and bosses,
> moose noses and tongues, beaver tails from
> the wooded country, the choicest venison, wild
> ducks and geese, fresh trout and whitefish, and
> a lavish spread of delicacies from the old world,
> brought by the Governor himself.

Following the banquet, "all hands were highly gratified with a Dance which Governor Simpson was pleased to entertain them with." Then the fiddlers played, the jigs and reels were whirled, the wines and spirits flowed into the night. For Moberly, such a night of revelry brought mixed blessings, when, after a few glasses of Hudson's Bay rum the new recruit had to take to his bed. The next morning "Sir George came to me and was good enough to place me on the sick list, with nothing to do until the return of the Saskatchewan brigade from York Factory."

The day after arrival was all business. Simpson gathered with his chief factors to hold the Council of the Northern Department, and for hours every day for several days, business for the coming year was decided on.

More than work had to be determined. As Letitia Hargrave commented, the end of the council was awaited with both hope and anxiety, for then "we will know where people are going & who are applauded & who admonished.... There are a great number of commissions to be given but we will not hear of them either till he [George Simpson] comes."

Moberly was astonished at the variety of men found at these gatherings: with the chief factors' entourages, passing brigades, and curious Natives, and as many as "500 men of various nationalities, Scotch, French-Canadian, Shetlander, Norwegians, half breeds, and heaven knows what else," and their women and children might gather. In the sun-filled warmth of high summer these were good times — leisure times, gala times, feasting times, playing times. It was a time to meet old friends. Time to gossip. Time for romance. Time to drink and fight. Something for everyone — so long as the brigades remained, the scene was one continuous festivity of eating, drinking, and fighting. For such revelry, the governor's visits were anticipated throughout The Great Fur Land, and the memories remained for a lifetime in the minds of those who experienced them.

Then, the Council's business done for another year, the multitudes dispersed to their far-flung posts and duties, the Natives to their forests. Simpson wasted no time in calling for his magnificent canoes and boatmen for the return to Lachine. As the canoes pulled away from the wharf, guns were fired, flags were waved, songs were sung, and cheers from master and men filled the air. Seventy-four years after such a departure, the event was still fresh in the memory of the then aged Moberly:

> We watched the great canoes, the flag of the Hudson's Bay Company proudly floating at each stern, the Iroquois crews chanting their boat songs, until they had turned the first point; then the men of the brigades became active in loading provisions and manning their boats.

The emperor gone, the national holiday over for another year, the great wheel of commerce commenced once more its monotonous grind.

Near the end of his travels, Simpson was accompanied by an old army colonel. It was a weary, wet journey over which the colonel refused to grumble. But later in his journal, he paid the ultimate compliment to Simpson as traveller: "Sir G. Simpson is the best traveller I ever fell in with, the very hardiest man I know. On service I can endure any hardship cheerfully, but I believe he is a glutton in that way, and prefers hardship to ease at any time."

And for Simpson? What was in it for him apart from his duty?

It was in his nature to prove his command over events. His illnesses, his fear of apoplexy, his eye troubles, even his growing old were kept at bay, it seems, for a while, at least, by travel. And so Simpson kept up these journeys till the end. "Forty times I passed over that ground," he would say with quiet pride, the poetry of the phrasing reflecting in memory the images of Sir William Butler, a western traveller:

> He who has once tasted the unworded freedom of the Western wilds must ever feel a sense of constraint within the boundaries of civilized life.... Nor can after-time ever wholly remove it; midst the smoke and hum of cities, midst the prayer of churches, in street or salon, it needs but little cause to recall again the wandering image of the immense meadows, where far away, at the portals of the setting sun, lies the Great Lone Land.

14

Last Years:
The Polite Old English Gentleman

I introduced myself to him and found him to be
the polite old English gentleman.
— William Senklar

To the popular mind in the mid-nineteenth century, the land of the fur trade was an unknown mystery, so when Canadian geologist Henry Youle Hind explored Rupert's Land, he was amazed by what he found:

> It appears that the operations of the Hudson's Bay Company extend over territories whose inhabitants owe allegiance to three different governments, British, Russian, and the United States. These immense territories exceeding 4,500,000 square miles in area, are divided for the exclusive

purposes of the fur trade, into four departments
and thirty-three districts, in which are included
one hundred and fifty-two posts, commanding
the services of three thousand agents, traders,
voyageurs, and servants, beside giving occasional
or constant employment to about one hundred
thousand Indian hunters. Armed vessels, both
sailing and steam, are employed on the North
West coast to carry on the fur trade with the warlike natives of that distant region.... History does
not furnish another example of an association of
private individuals exerting a powerful influence
over so large an extent of the earth's surface, and
administering their affairs with such consummate skill and unswerving devotion to the original objects of the incorporation.

To add to Hind's astonishment, those forty years were a
period of unparalleled peace in Company domains. As the mid-
twentieth-century politician and writer Grant MacEwan put it,
Simpson "ruled for nearly 40 difficult years without any major
trouble in Rupert's Land. That record speaks for itself." Similarly,
Arthur Morton recalled that the 1857 Select Committee "pre-
possessed that the Company was the government of a continental domain ... found it hard to grasp the fact that it did not govern," yet the HBC territories were "a vast domain ... wrapped in
profound peace."

The officer masterminding this operation with such consummate skill and unswerving devotion was, of course, Sir
George Simpson, a man seen on the streets of Montreal as the
polite old English gentleman. It would have been difficult for

those Montrealers to comprehend that such a man controlled the vast empire described by Hind. They would have been amazed at how Simpson did it, for the same reason that baffled Colin Robertson in 1821 — the ease with which Simpson got things done.

Those territories were all governed out of his headquarters in Lachine, just west of Montreal. During the summer he made an annual trip to Rupert's Land for the meeting of the Council. By the 1840s and 50s the Council had become supreme. Known as the Council of the Northern Department, it assumed a general authority over all other departments, and served, because of its colonial status, as both legislative assembly and executive council.

Simpson did not have supreme authority during those few days of Council. Any decision Simpson had made in the previous year had to be approved by Council, but after thirty-seven years, Simpson could say, "They could outvote me, but it has never been so."

Perhaps his greatest accomplishment in dealing with his officers was to instill into them a sense of service to the Company. Before Simpson, officers had been self-serving and independent. By Simpson's last years his men were so dedicated that their lives were freely bound to the Company with the greatest pride. A century after Simpson, it was enough for officers to write proudly on their tombstones that they had served the Honourable Hudson's Bay Company. It was this above all that permitted the Company to be so successful in the late nineteenth and early twentieth century, placing it beyond the ordinary — an "icon," the papers now call it. If Simpson's pride of service does not now shine as brightly, perhaps to that can be attributed the slow decline in the Company's fortunes.

* * *

George Simpson had wintered at Montreal as early as 1826, when he had been appointed to the Southern Department. The circumstances of his marriage, his illness, and his trip around the world had all made his residence there sporadic. Nevertheless, Montreal was becoming an important seat of business for him, requiring his stay there for longer periods.

In the early 1830s, the Company purchased a three-storey mansion for Simpson's residence in Lachine called Hudson's Bay House, right on the canal from whence the annual brigades would start for the Indian territories. Its impressive portico led into a central hall. On the right was Simpson's office, and behind, the office of his secretary, Edward Hopkins. Across

Hudson's Bay House, Sir George Simpson's residence in Lachine, Quebec.

the hall was the great salon, running the depth of the building, fifty-five feet long. Here, Simpson entertained, the room filled with his dining-room set embossed with the family motto ALIS NUTRIOR — "I am fed by my wings" — aptly suiting the peripatetic governor. Everywhere on the walls, Simpson displayed the Native artifacts he had collected on his many travels across North America.

With the return of Simpson's family from Red River to London in 1833, Simpson's home life underwent a drastic change from that envisaged in 1830. There would be no capital of Rupert's Land at Red River, no lady presiding over Government House; the most powerful governor in the British Empire would keep his residence, not within his domain, but in London, England, or Lachine, in Canada, and he would visit the land of his governance only once a year to preside over his Council.

As well as the apoplexy that had threatened Simpson's life in the early thirties, the governor, about 1838, developed another problem that threatened to bring an end to his career — his eyesight began to fail. As early as 1840, Letitia Hargrave saw him and commented that "his eyes dont look bad, but when he signs his name he has to turn them away from the paper." But Mrs. Webster, close to the family of Geddes Simpson, observed that "the Governor is in a very precarious state of health, and ... the violent medicine given him for his eyes is doing his constitution harm and his sight no good."

Simpson's response to this new threat to his mobility was to pick up the pace. He found a curious "cure" for his eye problems — travel. Through travel, he found, his illnesses seemed to vanish. His difficulty in writing was met by hiring a shorthand clerk. This was the dapper Edward Hopkins, twenty-one years of age in 1841, who now became Simpson's secretary and most trusted attendant.

Frances's misfortunes with her pregnancies continued, each with a threat to her own life and that of the child. The birth of Augusta D'Este in 1841 was a difficult cross-breach that nearly took the lives of both mother and child. As a consequence, Augusta suffered from epilepsy, which prevented her from living a normal life.

It was to that situation that Simpson returned to London in October 1842, fresh from his journey round the world. It had been his intention to settle in Lachine with his whole family in 1843, but with the illness of the child and the health of the mother, the move had to be postponed. So in the spring of 1843, Simpson once again returned to Lachine alone, while back in London, Frances gave birth to her fourth child in September of 1843, a healthy girl named Margaret Mackenzie Simpson.

In 1848, Simpson met Angus Cameron, the nephew of Chief Factor Angus Cameron, who had asked Simpson to help his nephew find employment in the banking world of Montreal. George promptly pronounced Angus "a fine, promising young man," set him up in a job with the Bank of Montreal, found him accommodation in a French household where he could learn that language, and took him under his wing to foster his career.

In turn, Angus warmed to his older mentor, and over a period of twelve years wrote letters to his uncle and relatives relating his experiences with the great governor. "Young Angus's letters," wrote Elaine Mitchell, the holder of the Cameron papers, "reveal Sir George as he appeared to a shrewd and discerning outsider, who, with every reason to be grateful to him, was yet no sycophant." They are enlightening reminiscences of Sir George Simpson as he was in the fourth decade of his power.

Simpson took Angus around the business circuit "for hours every day he was in town, to the Banks Law offices and wherever he had to do business — he always asked me to walk in saying that nothing need be private to me, introduced me where I was not known, &c." Naturally, Angus appreciated Simpson's help as he rose in the banking community of the city, but what he liked most about Simpson was his friendliness and easy manner:

> He has never been otherwise than full of the greatest Kindness to me, always the hand extended when I met him and the cheerful smile & the jocular remark, giving one as reserved as I am & that's not a little, ample opportunity for advancement.... I can talk to him with the same familiarity I would to you; tell him all my mind as regards office &c.

But if Angus thought he could avoid telling anything, he was soon met with one of Simpson's techniques of gathering information: "If one does not tell freely he will have it by questioning, & such questions as he does ask."

Angus noted that Simpson "has a happy knack of making those around him (if he likes them) feel so too." Angus was called nothing but "friend Cameron," and ten years after their meeting, Simpson remained "as well and jolly as ever." If he had a fault, "Sir G. is a man who can enjoy a laugh at another's cost, but not one to like to be laughed at." (A fault of most people.) And while Simpson remembered a man's good qualities, he did not readily forget his failings — not a bad quality in a governor who had to make postings over a vast domain.

For a man who had been in power thirty-eight years, Angus noticed a remarkable thing: "Finlayson has more pride in his little finger than Sir George has about him all ... nor would I give Sir George for dozens of him." Although Angus came in time to respect Duncan Finlayson, "still I would not give Sir George for him yet."

Angus and Sir George disagreed twice on important matters, but in each case it ended happily for their relationship. When Angus was offered a position with the new Bank of Toronto, Sir George thought the offer was to induce him to make a large deposit with the new bank. Angus was offended, grumbling, "I am too proud to allow him suppose that I cannot get forward without his assistance."

A more serious matter arose when Angus and Simpson's daughter Frances fell in love, and Angus presented his suit. Simpson wrote to Angus Sr. to explain his position:

> Your nephew Angus has stood very high in my regard ever since I became acquainted with him; and as he seems to have made himself agreeable to my Daughter, I did not withhold my consent, altho' his position in Life, was not such as (considering my circumstances) I might have looked for in a Son in Law.

Again, young Angus was upset. He let Simpson know that he would never have asked Fanny to marry him if he had not seen his way clearly without any help. In both these cases, Simpson accepted his defeat and bore no grudge. The day before the wedding, Simpson handed Cameron a check for $1,000. Fanny and Angus settled in Toronto, where their first child, George Simpson Cameron, was born. Sir George went to Toronto to stand as godfather. In turn, the Camerons became friends with up-and-coming doctor James Thorburn and his wife, Jane Mackenzie McTavish. Jane was George's granddaughter, daughter of his first-born child, Maria Louisa. In this way, George was reunited with one of his long-ago London children and they became his second family in Canada.

Cameron's letter tells us something else about Simpson. He had a curiously simple way of speaking that may have had something to do with his Gaelic-speaking origins. These peculiarities of speech so struck Cameron that he recorded a few of them for posterity. When Chief Factor Cameron was defrauded by a certain Mr. McKay, who had absconded to the United States, Simpson did not think it worth the time and money to pursue the man: "McKay is a scamp and ever was … a great scamp, a great scamp — were I in your Uncle's place I would allow him to go to H - - -."

And once, when George was ill and Cameron inquired after his health, Simpson responded, "Oh, it's d- - - -d bad, they keep me drink-outed — I am not able to smoke or do anything else."

Elaine Mitchell's view of George Simpson is of a warm humanitarian, whose kindness, consideration, and jollity were marked features of his character:

> Simpson's appetite for business was the excite-
> ment and satisfaction which an enthusiastic,
> energetic and restless man, of great executive
> ability and large views, must feel in reorganiz-
> ing and directing a giant concern. Intelligent,

shrewd and realistic, with an intense and catholic curiosity, a genius for detail, an optimistic temperament and the art of getting along with all kinds of people, he had the good fortune to inherit a still soundly-based, if temporarily demoralized, empire which his talents and enterprise were to revivify and preserve for a greater future. His faults, like those of most men, were the excesses of these virtues. Ambitious and worldly he was, but not, in my view, primarily self-seeking, so there was always room in his life for the "Man of Feeling" to show itself.

With Lady Simpson's return to Lachine in 1845, life fell into a familiar routine as the years progressed. With the coming of spring, the bustle began with the hiring of the recruits, the preparation of the indents for the high country, and the spring dispatches arriving from England, those to be sent to the far-flung territories. Then, with the end of the bustle, Simpson prepared for his own journey to the Southern and Northern councils, taking with him his secretary, Edward Hopkins, and his manservant, James B. Murray. Suddenly, a quiet monotony fell on Hudson's Bay House. With George away, Frances found, "we lead a very quiet life just now, seldom going beyond the door." Frances was pleased with George's return in the late summer, because then "he is so well known to every body that we have constant invitations to go out, or else people here, which breaks the monotony of the life we live."

In the summer months, of course, with the calm settling over the house, Frances's social life might have been curtailed, but could not have been as monotonous as claimed. Her sister Isobel Finlayson was there to afford her daily company. And close by lived the painter Annie Hopkins, wife of Edward, so that during the summer the three would have had the opportunity for many quiet get-togethers. Certainly, when George returned from the Northwest, Edward and Annie were regular Sunday guests at the Simpson table. The pleasant rural village of Lachine with the lovely river close by would have given the women many opportunities for pleasant summer walks. As the wife of the governor, so well-known in Montreal society, invitations to visit would certainly have come from the ladies of quality who knew her. It could not have been as monotonous as Frances suggests, but does point to the pleasure with which Frances looked forward to the lively scene when George was home, when Montreal social life continued through the long winters.

The establishment at Lachine was run on a strict discipline. The entire staff and families met for breakfast, but then social life ended until the end of the working day. This was a system

Canoe and voyageurs passing a waterfall. Watercolour by Frances Ann ("Annie") Hopkins, 1869.

Frances knew well. She had lived it day by day for her entire life prior to her marriage. It was the routine of the broker's counting house now imposed on Hudson's Bay House.

During this period, the apoplexy that had periodically stricken George Simpson continued with its usual severity. As early as 1847, Letitia again reported that "Mrs. Colville shocked me by the information that he has of late had two very severe apoplectic seizures & that being aware that he may die at any moment he had set his family affairs in order before he left Lachine for Moose [Factory]."

In September of 1849, Lady Simpson became pregnant with her fifth child, and the difficulties she had experienced with earlier pregnancies recurred. As her confinement drew near, her health became critical. Letitia Hargrave wrote: "Lady Simpson was to be confined in a few weeks & had been very ill, so much so that they had great fears about her. Sir George ... had made arrangements with their [doctor's] wife that Lady S. should live in their house in Montreal during the time." And there, on June 14, 1850, a long-awaited son was born. He was named John Henry Pelly Simpson in honour of John Henry Pelly, the long-serving London governor of the HBC.

The joyous birth of a son was followed by the last sad event in the life of Frances. Somehow Frances had contracted tuberculosis. Gradually the illness grew and after several years of suffering, Frances died on March 21, 1853, one week short of her forty-first birthday. She was buried in the newly opened Mount Royal Cemetery in Montreal.

Her death was a blow from which Simpson suffered greatly. In June 1852, Peter Skene Ogden wrote, "I regret to say that Sir Geo. is in a poor state of health and is very much reduced and looks very ill."

The people of Hudson's Bay House were "truly distressed and none more so than the bereaved husband himself who feels his loss keenly," reported Duncan Finlayson. Later that same year, when George stopped at Sault Ste. Marie, where the Hargraves were living, Letitia thought he looked "worn and old."

The death of Frances was to usher in the last phase of Simpson's life; it was now autumn — the growing old, the dying off. His wife was only one of many of Simpson's companions who were to leave the world during those years. In England, his beloved Uncle Geddes had died in 1849, Uncle Duncan in 1855, and William Scott, Simpson's friend since 1808, in 1856. His mentor and closest friend, Andrew Colvile, died in the same year. Simpson became aware that to return to England to retire would leave him as alone there as in Montreal. He visited England in the winter of 1855–56, and mentioned this to his friend, Chief Factor Angus Cameron:

> I deeply sympathize with you in your family affliction, which indeed has been very great: I too have been sorely tried in that way, and in this country where I at one time had many relatives and friends, they are now (by the Sweeping Hand of Death) reduced to so small a number, that here, comparatively speaking, I am quite a Stranger.

It was probably this fact that convinced Sir George to stay in Canada. The young Angus Cameron wrote, "I am inclined to think that Sir George will never leave Canada. The monument he is having placed in the new cemetery in Montreal will cost £1,000, and that he has chosen the prettiest spot there." And later he added, "I think Sir George will never go home. He sends home the children this Autumn, but Hopkins tells me he himself has no intention of leaving Canada."

So Simpson stayed on in Canada. It was, after all, not an unpleasant life. He continued the governorship of the Company, his authority never challenged by subordinates or the Committee in London. He was forever busy in a whirl of social gatherings. He kept a stable of fine horses and a wine cellar, which gave him great pride. This period in his life was to make Simpson's fortune. He was now one of the best-known men of business and society in Montreal. He continued to serve on boards, invested in properties and businesses, and made investments in banking, railways, steamships, and real estate that would span the Canadas, the United States, and the United Kingdom.

Simpson's interest in his traders was never neglected. As early as 1826 he had been approached by several of his officers to invest their money for them. Simpson accepted the charge. He had continued to do so over the years, until by the 1850s his investments for his officers had become so great a part of his duties that a small fee was charged. But for many years this had been done gratuitously by Simpson, and his wise investments had gained him the trust of his traders.

It was at this time that Simpson had the only photograph taken of him that has been found. It expresses all of this — the man satisfied with his power, yet showing the weariness that the years had placed upon him. Simpson was growing old, and he knew it. Still, he recognized another truth about himself:

Altho' work now becomes irksome to me at times, I scarcely think I would be perfectly

happy unless I had something to attend to in
the counting house, however independent my
circumstances might be.

*The only known photograph of Sir George Simpson, taken in Montreal,
Quebec, mid-1850s.*

In his private and confidential letter of March 12, 1859, to the London governor, Henry H. Berens, Simpson only suggested his retirement:

> In February next I shall have completed Forty years connexion with the Hudson's Bay [Company], I trust, creditably to myself and advantageously to the concern. During that very long period, I have never been off duty for a Week at a time, nor have I ever allowed Family considerations or personal convenience to come in competition with the claim I considered the Company to have had on me. After completing Forty Years "in harness" I have had it in contemplation to tender my resignation. It will occasion me regret to sever my ties with the Company, by whom I have been treated with a degree of liberality and consideration for which I shall ever feel most thankful. From the Board of Direction I have had uniform support, in my official capacity & from its individual members I have experienced great kindness and personal attention. It is nearly high time however that I rested from incessant labour; moreover, I should be disinclined to hold an appointment when I could no longer discharge its duties to my own entire satisfaction. I shall soon therefore make way for some younger man who I trust may serve the Company as zealously & conscientiously as I have done.

Simpson went on, hinting at retirement, but never quite taking the final step.

In the winter of 1860, Simpson suffered two more attacks of apoplexy from which he seemed to recover as usual. In the spring he attempted to journey to Red River by railway, but turned back at St. Paul, Minnesota, fearing that if he continued, he would "leave [his] bones in the prairies."

These harbingers were put aside in the summer with the arrival of the eighteen-year-old Edward, Prince of Wales, who was in Montreal to open the new Victoria Bridge. Simpson thrilled the young prince with a dramatic canoe display, which "afforded a most agreeable holiday to several thousand people who were enabled to witness the scene from the shore of the noble St. Lawrence."

That would be the last of George Simpson's achievements. Three days later, on September 1, while returning from Montreal to Lachine by carriage, he suffered a recurrence of his apoplexy. He was carried into Hudson's Bay House, where a bed was prepared for him in the salon on the first floor. There he remained for the next seven days. Later, his secretary, Edward Hopkins, would swear, "I have not the least doubt, and can say positively, that his mind was calm and sound and that he was in full possession of his mental faculties."

On the morning of the seventh day, his manservant, James Murray, held up a cup to offer a drink, which George accepted with pleasure. "Bless you my boy," Simpson uttered, and these, Murray said later, were Sir George's last words. With that, Simpson fell into another sleep and expired soon after, between ten and eleven o'clock in the morning of September 7, 1860. He was sixty-eight years of age.

Later, the three doctors would disagree on the cause of death. One diagnosed "inflammation of the brain," another "a fit of epilepsy, threatening apoplexy," and a third "hemorrhagic apoplexy, attended with epileptiform convulsions."

Asked how Sir George Simpson met his end, Edward Hopkins responded, "Wonderfully so for a man at the point of death."

Epilogue: Blaze of Glory

George Simpson was of the kind of which great
generals, ambassadors and courtiers, and
captains of industry are made, and he succeeded.
He has never had a successor fit to fill the place
he left vacant forty years after.
— Isaac Cowie, 1900

Simpson's body was carried from Hudson's Bay House by the Iroquois voyageurs who had carried him across the continent. Many of Montreal's most prominent citizens filled the cathedral for his funeral. As many as one hundred carriages followed his body to Mount Royal Cemetery. There his body was put to rest on a pleasant hillside facing north toward the distant Laurentian Hills, beyond which Rupert's Land began, and the beginnings of Simpson's "thick wood" forests that led ever farther into the vast expanse he had governed, even to the Arctic, which Mackenzie had reached so long before.

In time, the burial place of the great governor was forgotten. But that, of course, was not to be the end of it. Perhaps Lieutenant Lefroy, far back in time, got it right after all — here was "a fellow whom nothing will kill."

Within a half-dozen years of Simpson's death, "civilization" began to arrive in Red River Settlement. The village of Winnipeg took shape a half-mile from Fort Garry. Hotels were built, liquor laws were relaxed, and beer parlours and billiard halls made their appearance. And so did the evils of free trade: "Indians may frequently be seen lying drunk and incapable on the highways and plains."

A newspaper, the *Nor'Wester*, was established. Paddle-wheelers appeared on the waterways, replacing the employment of the voyageurs. And the lords of the plains, the Métis, saw the writing on the wall, and did not like it, and within the decade of Simpson's death their long-awaited uprising was in progress. In 1869 the charter of the HBC was surrendered to Canada in "probably the greatest single transfer of territory ever accomplished unheralded by war." With it, the old Colony of Assiniboia was squared off to become the province of Manitoba.

In 1863, the old members of the London Committee, so familiar to Simpson, sold their stock in a block to the International Financial Society, which turned its attention to land and store sales. Simpson's commissioned officers in time became no more than paid employees.

By the twenty-first century, nothing much is left of the old Company but its sales shops, magnificent edifices though they are, and offshoots which have become little more than big box stores. Its heart was torn out in 1986 when its Northern Stores was sold off. The new company, ironically calling itself the North West Company and claiming a four-hundred-year history, now flourishes with a virtual monopoly across northern Canada, from Nunavut and Labrador to the westernmost outposts of Alaska. Its breathtaking sweep would please Simpson.

Though the HBC still claims a rich history, it wobbles off into an uncertain future. That's not the way George Simpson left it. Perhaps if the old Company has lasted as long as it has, it is due in large part to the pride of service that Simpson instilled in its employees. Its failure may just come when that legacy is finally forgotten.

In the course of this narrative, I have given the opinions of many men and women who have attempted to define Simpson the man. They varied widely. Letitia Hargrave saw little more than "a good-natured, happy looking, dumpy man"; Malcolm McLeod saw a man "who ever combined the *suaviter in modo, et fortiter in imperio* [mild in manner, bold in command]." Two very different takes on the same man.

The Sixth Earl of Selkirk admired how Simpson could tell at a glance what men were good for. Mitchell extols his "ability to get along with all sorts of people," McKay his "profound understanding of men," Sale how he "could put great ideas into practice," and biographer Arthur Morton, Simpson's ability "to meet future dangers by remedies applied to the present."

Simpson himself claimed that "command only requires a spirit of enterprize," that a leader must have "public spirit and general view towards the welfare and good government of the place." We have seen Simpson's anger at corrupt Californians who abused their power to plunder a state's resources and oppress its people, his admiration for the simple Sandwich Islanders attempting to take control of their own destiny, and his disgust for Russia's brutal police.

Historian E.E. Rich, who gave more thought to it than most men, pointed to Simpson's "lack of airs," his "great confidence," his "early passion for travel as a set way of life," a "mind which could see the interaction of one problem with another," a "discipline ... in the enactment and enforcement of obviously sane rules." From these simple precepts, Rich maintains, came "such prosperity as the Company had never yet seen." These are all eminently sane assessments, none of them particularly startling, all leading in different directions, but suggesting great complexity.

In the end, of course, there is more — something inexplicable. Historian Chester Martin refers to it as Simpson's mysterious efficiency. Of course, he's right. We can no more confine Simpson's greatness to words than we can explain the final genius of Shakespeare or Beethoven.

About all we can say in the end is this: from an ordinary man, great things came.

When Simpson died, it is said, he was the dean of governors in British North America. Except for their remembrance in the names of schools, towns, and counties, those other governors have long passed into history. But not George Simpson. There is a public consciousness, some understanding that somehow he stands apart from those others, something that cannot quite be forgotten. Although a colonial governor, his powers did not vary much from those of a modern Canadian prime minister operating in a parliament. His "parliament" was the Council of the Northern Department, his "parliamentarians" the chief factors of the HBC, the restraint on both the Governor and Committee in London. Both the Council and the Committee could have removed Simpson at any time, but as he said near the end, "it has never been so."

It has often been pointed out that Simpson's career depended on the blind goddess — Fortune. Certainly we cannot deny the fortunate friendship of Andrew Colvile, the unexpected commission *locum tenens*, the capture of Colin Robertson, which gave him his opportunity in the Athabasca, and the timely coalition that placed Simpson as the most acceptable candidate. But against that we have the Chester Martin riposte: "Few have ever seized fortune with more briskness and audacity."

The ability to maintain power and to govern well places Simpson in a category by himself. As governor under the Charter of 1670, Simpson was both superintendent of a vast commercial enterprise and the political leader of Rupert's Land, a colony with all the powers of a modern state to enact laws and enforce them. Simpson fulfilled the obligations of the charter to an extraordinary degree. Taken all in all, the *Dictionary of National Biography* probably got it right in 1912 when it declared, "Simpson's work as administrator of the Hudson's Bay Company's Territories ... was coincident with the growth and progress which entitles him to be considered one of the architects of the present Canadian dominion."

Geographically, what is today modern Canada is far more the old Rupert's Land and the Indian Territories — Simpson's realm — than it is the old Canadas. It is difficult to imagine how, without Simpson, either Canada or the colonial office or the HBC could have had influence enough to preserve the West Coast from American annexation. Without Simpson's able governance, it is difficult to imagine a Canada from sea to sea.

The dream of the unity of British North America from Atlantic to Pacific began with the voyages of Mackenzie in 1789 and 1793, and ended a century later in its fulfillment, with the completion of the railway in 1886. The dream begun by Sir Alexander Mackenzie was continued by Sir George Simpson and completed by Sir John A. Macdonald. Mackenzie left a record of possibility, Simpson of accomplishment, and Macdonald of fulfillment. These three men stood head and shoulders above others in their field. These three, their continuity clearly defined, deserve more than any others the title "Makers of Canada."

If glory includes amongst its many meanings (as it does) "praise, honor, or distinction extended by common consent," Simpson's career, taken all in all, must be one of the most distinguished ever led by a Canadian. In that context, Simpson's old friend and fellow trader J.D. Cameron spoke the perfect eulogy — Sir George Simpson's light had gone out, "just as he basked in a final blaze of glory."

Chronology of
Sir George Simpson (1792–1860)

Compiled by D.T. Lahey

Sir George Simpson	*Canada and the World*
	1670 May 2: the Hudson's Bay Company is created in London, with charter rights to exclusive trade in Rupert's Land.
1759 October 9: George Simpson, father of Sir George Simpson, is born in Avoch, Scotland.	**1759** General James Wolfe defeats the French at the Plains of Abraham; France will cede Canada to the British in 1763.
1776 George senior is established in Dingwall as a writer (lawyer).	**1776** The American Revolutionary War begins.
	1779 The NWC is formed in Montreal.
	1783 The American Revolutionary War. Thousands of Loyalists go into exile to what would become

Sir George Simpson	*Canada and the World*
	Ontario, New Brunswick, and Nova Scotia, and the beginnings of Canada.
	1789 July 14: The French Revolution begins with the storming of the Bastille. On the same day Alexander Mackenzie, later Sir Alexander, reaches the Arctic Ocean after exploring the Mackenzie River.
1792 George Simpson is born in Scotland, likely in or near the town of Dingwall.	
	1793 May 9: Alexander Mackenzie leaves Fort Fork on the Peace River to find a way to the Pacific Ocean. In June the Reign of Terror begins in France.
	July 22: Mackenzie reaches the Pacific Ocean at Dean Channel near the village of Bella Coola. He is the first European to cross the North American continent north of Mexico.
	1802 Napoleon becomes Consul for Life.

Sir George Simpson

Canada and the World

1803
Alexander Mackenzie publishes his *Voyages* from Montreal to the Pacific, in which he proposes a united British fur trade from coast to coast. Beethoven writes his *Eroica* symphony.

1805
George Simpson senior is known to be living in Dingwall, Scotland. He is appointed to the position of Agent to the British Fisheries Society in Ullapool in northern Scotland.

George Simpson is attending school in Dingwall.

1805
October 22: Horatio Nelson wins the Battle of Trafalgar, but dies of a bullet wound.

1808
George Simpson, aged sixteen, completes his Dingwall schooling and leaves for London to begin a seven-year apprenticeship in the sugar trade.

1808
Wellington invades Spain beginning the Peninsular War against Napoleon. It will continue until 1814.

1811
Thomas Douglas, Fifth Earl of Selkirk, is granted a large territory called Assiniboia, at the forks of the Assiniboine and Red River (modern Winnipeg).

1815
Simpson completes his apprenticeship as a sugar broker. He is known to be carrying out duties for the Hudson's Bay Company.

1815
January 11: John A. Macdonald, future first prime minister of Canada, is born in Glasgow, Scotland.

Sir George Simpson

He visits the Poolers in Reigate.

October 22: Simpson's his first child, Maria Louisa, is born.

1820–21
February 28: George Simpson is sent to North America as governor *locum tenens*; in July he takes command of the Athabasca campaign.

1821
George Simpson is appointed governor of the Northern Department.

Canada and the World

June 18: Wellington defeats Napoleon at Waterloo, Belgium. Napoleon is sent into exile on the Island of St. Helena in the South Atlantic.

1819–22
John Franklin explores the Arctic coast west of the Mackenzie River.

1820
March 12: Sir Alexander Mackenzie dies in Scotland.

April 8: Thomas Douglas dies in France.

John A. Macdonald and his family leave Scotland to settle in Canada.

1821
John Franklin's second exploration of the Arctic, east of the Mackenzie River.

March: The HBC and the NWC amalgamate to form a single fur-trading company under the name Hudson's Bay Company.

May 5: Napoleon dies, aged 51, on St. Helena.

September 3–4: Michael Faraday discovers the principle of

Sir George Simpson

1822–23
Simpson restructures the Company's operations in Rupert's Land.

1824–25
Simpson travels overland to the Pacific to restructure Company operations there, then returns to Rupert's Land.

1828
Simpson travels through New Caledonia and shoots the Fraser Canyon. He is accompanied by his wife, Margaret Taylor.

1829
Simpson returns to England to marry his cousin, Frances Simpson.

1830–33
February 24, 1830. George Simpson marries Frances Ramsay Simpson. He returns to Rupert's Land with his bride and settles at Red River. The family suffers as tragedy strikes their first-born and Frances falls critically ill. In 1833, Simpson takes Frances back to England.

Canada and the World

electro-magnetic rotation — the principle behind the electric motor.

1824
Beethoven composes his *Choral Symphony*.

1828
Beethoven dies in Vienna.

1830
September 15: The Liverpool and Manchester Railway opens; the first locomotive passenger service is started. The line proves the viability of rail transport, and large-scale railway construction begins in Britain and spreads quickly throughout the world. The railway age begins.

1831
August 29: Michael Faraday discovers electro-magnetic induction, the principle behind

Sir George Simpson

Canada and the World

the electric transformer and generator, allowing electricity to be turned from a scientific curiosity into a powerful technology.

1832
Simpson writes his "Character Book."

April 22: George's son, George Geddes, dies at Red River.

1833
Simpson takes his wife Frances back to England.

1834
Dickens adopts the pen name "Boz."

1835
Simpson authorizes the Dease-Simpson Arctic Discovery Expedition. He returns to Canada and makes Lachine, Quebec, his new headquarters.

1836
Dickens publishes the first chapters of *The Pickwick Papers*.

1837
Dease and Simpson explore westward to Point Barrow, closing the exploration of the western Arctic coast of North America.

1837
June 20: Victoria is crowned Queen of England.

Rebellion breaks out in Upper and Lower Canada.

Sir George Simpson

1838
Simpson travels to Russia to negotiate a treaty with the Russian America Company for control of part of the Alaska Panhandle.

1839
Dease and Simpson explore the eastern Arctic coast of North America to within sight of the Boothia Peninsula.

1841
January 25: Simpson is knighted by Queen Victoria to become Sir George Simpson.

March 3: Simpson leaves London to begin his journey around the world.

1842
Simpson takes up the cause of Hawaiian independence. In October he returns to England, completing his round-the-world journey.

Canada and the World

1840
July 4: the Cunard Line begins transatlantic operations.

1845
Sir John Franklin leaves England on his ill-fated expedition to find the North West Passage.

Sir George Simpson

Canada and the World

1846
John Rae explores Committee Bay.

1854
John Rae crosses the Boothia
Peninsula to discover the fate of
the Franklin Expedition.

1857
Simpson appears before the
Parliamentary Select Committee
in London.

1859
Simpson travels the Minnesota
Route to open a new way to
Rupert's Land.

1859
Charles Darwin publishes *Origin
of the Species*.

1860
July: Simpson must turn back
from his second trip to Rupert's
Land via Minnesota.

1860
HRH Edward visits Canada
to open the Victoria Bridge in
Montreal.

August: Simpson entertains HRH
Edward, Prince of Wales.

Charles Dickens publishes *Great
Expectations*.

September 1: Simpson falls
ill. He dies a week later, on
September 7.

1863
The HBC is sold to the
International Financial Society.

1867
Canada created by
Confederation.

Sir George Simpson

Canada and the World

1869
The first Riel Rebellion takes
place.

1870
Rupert's Land is transferred
to Canada; the Province of
Manitoba is formed; HBC gains
huge land tracts for settlement.

1872
British Columbia joins
Confederation, dependent on the
construction of a railway to the
Pacific.

1885
The Last Spike is driven in, and
Canada is finally joined from
coast to coast by a railway.

1905
The provinces of Alberta and
Saskatchewan are created, completing provincial representation
from sea to sea.

Further Reading

Borer, Mary Cathcart. *The City of London: A History.* New York: D. McKay Co., 1978.

Clunn, Harold P. *The Face of London.* London: Spring Books, 1970.

Cree, Muriel R. "Three Simpson Letters." *The British Columbia Historical Quarterly* Vol. 1, 1937: 115–21.

Dunlop, Jean. *The British Fisheries Society, 1786–1893.* Edinburgh: John Donald Publishers, 1978.

Dunlop, Jean. *The Clan Mackenzie: Independence in the North.* Edinburgh: Johnson and Baker, 1963.

Gauci, Perry. *Emporium of the World: The Merchants of London, 1660–1800*. London and New York: Hambleton, 2007.

Gauci, Perry. *The Politics of Trade: The Overseas Merchant in State and Society, 1660–1720*. Oxford: Oxford University Press, reprinted 2003.

Graham, Sir Frederick Ulric. *Notes of a Sporting Expedition in the Far West of Canada, 1847*. London: Printed for private circulation only, 1898.

Hancock, David. *The Citizens of the World: London Merchants and the Integration of the British Atlantic Community, 1735–1785*. Cambridge: Cambridge University Press, 1995. Essential reading for the training of an overseas merchant.

Hargrave, Joseph James. *Red River*. Montreal: J.J. Hargrave, 1871. Still good for the history of Red River immediately after the death of George Simpson.

Hargrave, Letitia. *The Letters of Letitia Hargrave*. Margaret Arnett Macleod, ed. Toronto: Champlain Society, 1947.

Johnson, Alice M. "Simpson in Russia." *The Beaver* (Summer 1960): 4–12. George's surprisingly tender relationship with his wife and daughter come across in his diary of his trip to Russia in 1838.

_____. "System and Regularity." *The Beaver* (Summer 1960): 36–39.

Johnson, Stephen M. "Wrangel and Simpson," *Old Trails and New Directions: Papers of the Third North American Fur Trade Conference.* Carol M. Judd and Arthur J. Ray, eds. Toronto: University of Toronto Press, 1980.

Kynaston, David. *The City of London: A World of Its Own, 1815–1890.* London: Chatto and Windus, 1994.

Lahey, Dale T. "The Case of the Vanishing Heiress." *Families,* 2002.

____. "How Old Was Sir George Simpson: An Exercise in the Genealogical Proof Standard." *Families: Journal of the Ontario Genealogical Society,* February 2006. Revised and privately published, 2007.

____. "The Strange Case of James K. Simpson." *Families, Journal of the Ontario Genealogical Society,* February 2010.

Martin, Chester. Introduction to *Journal of Occurrences in the Athabasca Department: By George Simpson, 1820 and 1821, and Report, Commonly Known as Simpson's Athabasca Journal.* Edited by E.E.Rich. HBRS, 1938.

MacKay, Douglas. *The Honourable Company: A History of the Hudson's Bay Company.* Indianapolis: Bobbs-Merrill, 1936. Still one of the best short histories of the Hudson's Bay Company.

Merk, Frederick. *Fur Trade and Empire: George Simpson's Journal Entitled Remarks Connected with the Fur Trade in the Course of a Voyage from New York Factory to Fort George and Back to York Factory, 1824–25, with Related Documents.* Cambridge, MA: Belknap Press of Harvard University Press, 1968.

Mitchell, Elaine Allen. "Sir George Simpson: 'The Man of Feeling.'" In Malvina Bolus, *People and Pelts: Selected Papers of the Second North American Fur Trade Conference.* Winnipeg: Peguis Press, 1972: 83–101.

Moberly, Henry John. *When Fur Was King.* In collaboration with William Bleasdell Cameron. Toronto: J.M. Dent, 1929. First presented in the 1921 issues of *The Beaver* under the title "Reminiscences of an HBC Fur Trade Factor."

Morton, Arthur S. *A History of the Canadian West to 1870–71: Being a History of Rupert's Land (The Hudson's Bay Company's Territory) and of the North West Territory (Including the Pacific Slope).* Second edition. Edited by Lewis G. Thomas. Toronto: University of Toronto Press, 1973.

Morton, W.L. "Donald A. Smith and Governor George Simpson." *The Beaver* (Winter 1978): 4–9.

Nute, Grace Lee. "Jehu of the Waterways." *The Beaver* (Summer 1960): 15–19.

Patterson, R.M. "We Clomb the Pathless Pass." *The Beaver,* Winter 1960.

Porter, Roy. *London: A Social History.* Cambridge, MA: Harvard University Press, 1994.

Rich, E.E. *The History of the Hudson's Bay Company 1670–1870, Volume Two 1763–1870.* London: HBRS, 1959. It is sometimes astonishing to read how Simpson could take the most adverse difficulty, and with a few tweaks, turn it the benefit of the Company. Rich is essential reading.

Robinson, Henry Martin. *The Great Fur Land: Or Sketches of Life in the Hudson's Bay Territory.* New York, Putnam's, 1879. Facsimile edition, Toronto: Coles Publishing, 1972.

Ross, Alexander. *The Fur Hunters of the Far West: A Narrative of Adventures in the Oregon and Rocky Mountains.* London: Smith, Elder, 1855, 2 volumes.

Saw, Reginald. "Treaty with the Russians." *The Beaver* (December 1948): 30–33.

Simpson, Frances. "Journey for Frances." Introduction by Grace Lee Nute. *The Beaver,* December 1953, March 1954, and June 1954.

Simpson, George. "The 'Character Book' of George Simpson, 1832," *Hudson's Bay Miscellany, 1670–1870.* HBRS: 1975.

Simpson, George. *Journal of Occurrences in the Athabasca Department: By George Simpson, 1820 and 1821, and Report, Commonly Known as Simpson's Athabasca Journal.* Toronto: The Champlain Society for the HBRS, 1938.

Simpson, George. *Narrative of a Journey Round the World in the Years 1841 and 1842, in Two Volumes.* London: Henry

Colburn, 1847. Difficult to find in modern libraries, but still worth a read.

Stevenson, John A. "Disaster at the Dalles." *The Beaver*, Vol. 22, No. 2 (September 1942): 19–21. Relates the tragic death of Simpson's daughter, Maria, in 1839.

Stewart, Susan. "Sir George Simpson: Collector." *The Beaver* (Summer 1982): 4–9.

West, John. *The Substance of a Journal During a Residence at the Red River Colony, British North America, and Frequent Excursions Among the North-West American Indians in the Years 1820, 1821, 1822, 1823.* London: L.B. Seeley, 1824. Johnson Reprint Corporation, 1966.

Williams, Glyndwr. "Family and Community in the Fur Trade." *The Beaver*, Autumn 1983.

Wilson, Clifford P. "The Emperor at Lachine." *The Beaver*, September 1934.

_____. "Sir George Simpson at Lachine." *The Beaver*, June 1934.

_____. "The Emperor's Last Days." *The Beaver*, December 1934. Wilson's articles are a little out of date now, and sometimes incorrect, but still offer a good overview.

Woodcock, George. "Grant, Cuthbert." *Dictionary of Canadian Biography Online.*

Acknowledgements

Many thanks to my wife, Peggy, for her encouragement to use genealogy to enrich my retirement days, opening for me, it sometimes seems, a never-ending world of riches, and to my son, Neil Lahey, for his careful reading of my manuscripts, accurate criticism, and everyday assistance in the final preparation of the text. Thanks also to Carroll Klein, Waterloo, editor emerita, for introducing me to the mysteries of text editing, and offering much practical advice and encouragement; Elinor Knight, genealogist, Guelph, for providing me with a woman's view against which to balance my opinions of Sir George; Judith Beattie, Keeper, HBCA (retired), for her careful reading and correction of my original manuscript; Carol Simpson, Winnipeg, for undertaking research for me at the HBC Archives in Winnipeg; Diane Baptie, my researcher in Scotland, for whom it seems there is no research problem for which she cannot find the answer. And finally, to the many descendants of Sir George Simpson who I have been privileged to know over the years, from whom I have received every assistance possible to fill in the story of Sir George and his more than six hundred descendants.

Index